Accou...
Partnerships

LEONARD E. STOKES

Professor of Accounting
Siena College

THOMSON
™
SOUTH-WESTERN

Australia · Canada · Mexico · Singapore · Spain · United Kingdom · United States

Accounting for Partnerships, 1e
Leonard E. Stokes

Editor-in-Chief:
Jack W. Calhoun

Vice President/Team Director:
Melissa S. Acuña

Senior Developmental Editor:
Sara E. Wilson

Production Editor:
Salvatore N. Versetto

Manufacturing Coordinator:
Doug Wilke

Compositor:
Navta Associates, Inc.

Printer:
Transcontinental Printing, Inc.
Louiseville, QC

Design Project Manager:
Michelle Kunkler

Cover and Internal Designer:
Ellen Pettengell Design
Chicago, Illinois

Cover Painting:
©2001 Frank Stella/Artists Rights
Society (ARS)
New York, New York

Media Developmental Editor:
Sally Nieman

Media Production Editor:
Robin K. Browning

Library of Congress Cataloging-in-
Publication Data
Stokes, Leonard E.
   Accounting for partnerships /
Leonard E. Stokes.
      p.   cm.
   Includes bibliographical references
and index.
      ISBN 0-324-12098-2 (alk. paper)
      1. Partnership--Accounting. 2.
Consolidation and merger of corpora-
tions--Accounting.
      I. Title.

HF5686.P225 S76 2002
657'.92--dc21   2002022368

BRIEF CONTENTS

CONTENTS

PREFACE

Today's educational environment is challenging for accounting educators. In addition to striving to be innovative as we provide our students with a technically appropriate curriculum, we are also working diligently to help them develop critical thinking, communication and life-long learning skills. *Accounting for Partnerships* has been created to help educators meet that challenge.

We understand that students learn best when content is made relevant and real to them. This text approaches the issues of partnership accounting with a unique narrative style. The reader is introduced to two CPAs, April and Leo, who think through the issues associated with forming a partnership, adding new partners, and liquidating the partnership. After developing a basic understanding of accounting for partnerships, the reader focuses on a very relevant and real consideration of the business world—"Taxation Issues Associated with Partnerships." For instructors who would like to provide the students with a more in-depth background of tax issues, this final chapter in the module provides straightforward, easy-to-understand coverage.

The end-of-chapter and other author-designed support materials for this module include class-tested materials for challenging the student's higher-level cognitive skills. Case studies and written research assignments are included in the end-of-chapter materials. The assignments, while relating to the stated learning objectives, also provide for various activities that provoke thinking, require writing, and include a range of difficulty levels. The Instructor's Resource Manual provides a rich assortment of ways in which the materials can be integrated to provide an active learning environment for all learning styles.

The South-Western Advanced Accounting Modular series allows instructors the flexibility of selecting specific topics for course coverage. Each easy-to-read module provides hands-on learning activities, research projects, and case studies. *Accounting for Partnerships* is one in a series of three modules. The other two modules include *Business Combinations and International Accounting*, by Herring (0-538-87893-2) and *Today's Essentials of Governmental and Not-for-Profit Accounting and Reporting*, by Martin and West (0-324-11164-9).

Key Features

Narrative Style: Two CPAs, April and Leo, are introduced in a manner that allows the students to follow the decision making process. These CPAs are designed to be identifiable by the students. Many students who are interested in emulating this path to success will be more inclined to read the technical material.

Flow-of-Transaction-Diagrams: Chapter 1 "Accounting for Partnership Formation, Operation, and Ownership Changes" uses innovative diagrams that can aid in visualizing the flow of assets and change in ownership.

Objective-Based Learning: The chapters were are designed around learning objectives. The objectives are stated in the beginning and are referenced throughout the reading. The chapter summaries are organized according to learning objectives with a specific narrative incorporated with each educational goal summarized so the student has obtained a connection with the learned material.

Integration of Material and Active Learning: The end-of-chapter material is designed to provide the students with an opportunity to apply the reading. The exercises and problems are referenced to the learning objectives. In addition, the Instructor's Resource Manual provides a variety of teaching tips designed by the author to integrate the material while providing an active learning environment for the course.

Assessing Understanding of the Material: The Instructor's Resource Manual provides tips on how the case studies and other assignments can be used as course embedded assessment tools. The manual includes a test bank that provides an assortment of multiple-choice questions, essays, and problems. Some of the class-tested questions provide the students with an opportunity to use their critical thinking skills.

Conceptual Questions and Interpretive Exercises: Partnership accounting provides the student with a fresh view of organizational formation, management structure, and information systems. Throughout the reader is provided with opportunities to think through alternative methods and ways to deal with the issues at hand.

Ties to the Real World: Partnerships exist as an exciting form of operation that most accountants will deal with during their professional careers. The text provides summaries from news articles and business publications that help bring this form of business structure to life.

Glossary: There is a comprehensive glossary defining the terms used throughout the three-chapter module.

Tax Issues: This module includes a separate chapter "Taxation Issues Associated with Partnerships." Taxation is one of the reasons for the formation of partnerships. The majority of accounting texts avoid many of the issues that make partnership accounting really interesting. This stand-alone chapter can be taught in as much depth as each instructor decides to include in his/her course. This chapter also allows institutions to increase tax coverage without adding an additional course.

Supporting Materials:

Instructor's Resource Manual (0-324-12985-8). This manual includes chapter outlines, teaching tips, solutions to assignments, and a Test Bank for each chapter. The author-created test bank items, which include multiple-choice, essay questions, and problems, provide a variety and range of difficulty levels to choose from. All are closely tied to the chapter learning objectives.

Acknowledgements

Appreciation is extended to Richard J. Campbell, University of Rio Grande, and Raymond Wacker, Southern Illinois University, for their assistance in the development of this text. Andrea Hotaling of Siena College was great to work with as she reviewed multiple drafts and provided her expertise to the creation of the end-of-chapter materials for the tax chapter. She was a needed friend throughout this project. Appreciation is extended to Sheila Viel, who solved, corrected and in many ways improved the end-of-chapter materials. To the outside reviewers of the chapters I want to give thanks for providing some great insight. I would also like to thank two of my colleagues at Siena College, Nancy Fittore, and Peggy Garnsey for critically reviewing different stages of the project.

I want to thank my family. Sue, Jennifer, and Stephen's love and support keep me going.

Leonard Stokes

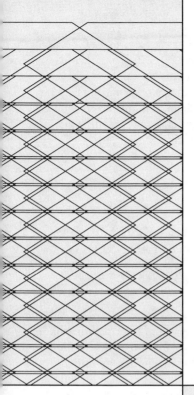

CHAPTER 1

ACCOUNTING FOR PARTNERSHIP FORMATION, OPERATION, AND OWNERSHIP CHANGES

LEARNING OBJECTIVES

- Discuss the legal issues associated with forming and operating a partnership.
- Determine a partner's capital balance when forming a partnership.
- Allocate partnership profits and losses.
- Compute a partner's capital balance when a partnership's ownership changes.

April and Leo are discussing their future. They are currently employed by an international accounting firm in a large metropolitan area. April, a CPA, has been working in the tax department and has acquired her own extensive tax library. Leo, also a CPA, has been working as an auditor for over eight years. Both have recently purchased their own state-of-the-art computers. After working together for several years, they have decided to start their own CPA firm. Although they both are on a partnership track with the firm, they would like the freedom to establish their own business based upon their choice of lifestyle. Their first issue is deciding what is the best form of an organization for their new business: a partnership or a corporation.

NATURE OF PARTNERSHIPS (LO 1)

This section will discuss the structure of a partnership and how it is formed. In addition, the discussion will compare and contrast a partnership and a corporate form of organization, including some legal and tax differences.

Partnership Defined

Many firms with more than two owners are formed as a partnership. Other organizations operate as a corporation. Corporations are structured based upon the laws in the state in which they are incorporated. A corporation can provide the benefit of limited liability. However, it does create a situation of double-taxation, where profits are taxed to the corporation and again to the owners upon the receipt of dividends. A partnership has less structure, and its earnings are only taxed once.

A **partnership** is an association of two or more individuals, or entities, that are in a legal profit-making operation. The profits from the partnership are **passed through** to the individual partners, who report the income on their individual tax returns. There is no tax on the partnership earnings themselves. The tax implications will be discussed further in Chapter 3. April and Leo like the income pass-through opportunities and have decided to structure their new company as a partnership.

Most states have accepted the **Uniform Partnership Act (UPA)** that defines the legal relationships between the partners, the partnership, and the community. The partners can establish their own **partnership agreement**, which acts as a contract to govern their operations. This agreement allows the partners to decide the purpose of their business, the powers and duties of the partners, and the procedures to be followed to determine their separate profit or loss interests. A partner's **profit interest** is his/her share of the profits (or losses) earned by the partnership. Partnerships that do not develop their own partnership agreement are governed by the UPA that requires *equal* distribution of profits and losses.

Legal Implications of a Partnership

Partnerships have some unique characteristics that distinguish them from corporations. Partners have a **mutual agency** relationship. That is, partners are agents of the organization who can enter into agreements in order to carry on the partnership's business. Mutual agency provides assurance to the community that the individual partners can legitimately carry out the partnership business and that contracts entered into by a partner on behalf of the partnership are legal and binding.

WOMEN PARTNERS IN PROFESSIONAL FIRMS

Partnerships are a common form of business for CPA and law firms. April is not alone as a female working for a large CPA firm: women make up almost half of the work force at the large CPA firms. The percentage of women partners has been growing and was reported to represent 11%, or 1,315, of 12,427 total partners at 17 of the top 25 CPA firms that participated in the *CPA Personnel Report's Annual Survey of Women in Public Accounting – 1999*.

Deloitte & Touche reported the highest percentage of female partners, and PricewaterhouseCoopers has the largest number of women partners. Large law firms reported 15% of the partners are women. However, in 1996 it was noted that half of the women were non-equity partners. Also, 66% of law partners under the age of 41 do not plan to retire with their present firms.

Accounting firms are being noted for taking the lead in professional services fields by creating cultures favorable for women. "Accounting firms realized there was tremendous turnover among their people. D&T was the first to really evaluate the lack of work/life balance, and the rest followed suit. All have worked aggressively to retain their women professionals. They all (Big-Five) realized that the burn-out model for the first 10 to 12 years of a career is not the most productive."

Both April and Leo are aware of the cultural changes taking place within the CPA firms. They enjoy the current environment, but they just want the opportunity to go on their own.

"Women Inch into Partnership," *Public Accounting Report*, September 15, 1999, Vol. 23. No. 17 pp. 1, 4.

In a general partnership, the partners have **unlimited liability** because they can be personally liable, jointly and severally, for the partnership's obligations. Due to the ease of forming partnerships, this additional liability on the partners provides recourse to individuals doing business with the partnership.

With regard to ownership, each partner has the right to dispose of his/her partnership interest. However, the individual acquiring the partnership interest is not a partner unless all of the remaining partners agree with the admission.

When a new partner is added or an existing partner leaves, retires, or dies, the partnership is assumed to have ended. This concept of **limited life** can be overcome through properly writing the partnership agreement to provide for continuation despite these occurrences.

Alternatives to a general partnership have become available in recent years. One of these, a **limited partnership**, must be made up of one or more general partners (who assume personal liability for the partnership debts) and some limited partners. The limited partners are at risk only for their investment or capital contributions. This structure is not appropriate for April and Leo since they both will be general partners and there will be no limited partners in their company. However, other choices are available to them.

They can consider organizing the partnership as an LLC or an LLP. A **limited liability company (LLC)** is a pass-through type entity that can be formed by one or more individuals. An LLC provides liability protection similar to that of a corporation. Many states don't allow professionals such as physicians, lawyers, or accountants to form LLCs. States do allow these professionals to set up their companies as **limited liability partnerships (LLPs)**, which make it possible to protect an individual partner's personal assets from malpractice of the other partners. However, the individual partner's assets are not protected from his/her own acts of professional malpractice. The partners are also responsible for partnership obligations that are treated the same as a normal partnership.

Non-professional partnerships can consider an **S-corporation**. An **S-corporation** is a pass-through entity that provides the owners the benefits of a corporation. S-corporations came about through changes in the tax code. As such, there are restrictions imposed by the tax regulations, especially with the number of stockholders, related to forming and operating an S-corporation.

◢ CONCEPTUAL QUESTION AND REFLECTION

Should April and Leo be happy with a partnership as their form of organization? Further information associated with this decision can be found by reading "C Corporation, LLC, or Sole Proprietorship? What Form Is Best for Your Business?" written by G. Fleischman and J. Bryant, *Management Accounting Quarterly*, Spring 2000, pp. 14 – 21, or "Twenty Questions on Selection of a Legal Entity" written by Peter A. Karl III, *The CPA Journal*, August 1999, pp. 40 – 45.

Underlying Operating Principles

April's and Leo's intent is to form a business whose operations they can control. The concept that the partnership is an entity that can own property and that the property contributed by the partners belongs to the partnership is supported by the *entity theory*. This theory views the organization as a distinct legal entity separate from the individual partners. Coupled with the entity theory is the *proprietary theory*, which supports the majority of partnership operations. The proprietary theory views the organization through its owners, the partners. Issues include:

- the unlimited liability of the partners,
- salaries being considered to be distributions to the partners (subject to self-employment taxes and not withholding taxes), and
- partnership income being considered taxable income to the partners and not subject to a partnership-level tax. (As discussed earlier, corporations are subject to double taxation.)

Corporations issue stock and have a balance sheet section titled *Stockholders' Equity*. Partners each have separate capital accounts representing their **capital interests**. These accounts do not have to be equal amounts between the partners, nor does the account have to be equivalent to the individual partner's **profit interest**.

Unlike corporate accounting, which is required to follow GAAP and, thus, must follow **accrual accounting** procedures, a partnership may use the **cash basis of accounting** if that fits its business purpose. Accrual basis accounting matches expenses and revenues to the proper periods. Cash basis accounting recognizes revenue when the cash is received and expenses when cash is paid. Organizations using the cash basis may be able to control the recognition of income. Since tax issues are a major reason for forming partnerships, the cash basis can be used to impact the timing of taxable income. The IRS requires taxpayers with inventories, other than certain small businesses with gross receipts less than $1 million, to use the accrual basis. Professional service firms, such as CPAs, can choose to use the cash basis.

Accounting for a partnership requires care in maintaining equality between the partners. The equality is based upon the terms of the partnership agreement. The partnership must maintain a fair accounting of the partners' capital accounts. This is important not only for financial reporting purposes but also related to the tax impact of distributions and issues associated with dissolving the partnership. The remainder of this chapter will discuss the unique accounting issues associated with forming and operating a partnership. Issues associated with dissolving and liquidating the partnership will be covered in Chapter 2, and tax issues will be discussed in Chapter 3.

BORDERS AND AMAZON.COM FORM A PARTNERSHIP

Corporations as well as individuals choose to form partnerships. Part of Amazon.com's business strategy is to form partnerships with brick-and-mortar companies. Companies such as Borders and Toys R Us have stopped running their own web-based businesses. They have partnered with Amazon who will run the website under the Borders name. Corporations may establish formal partnerships, or they may choose alternative reporting structures such as joint ventures. Regardless of the form, the substance is two or more corporations being cooperative in one venture while potentially being competitive in others.

ACCOUNTING FOR PARTNERSHIP ACTIVITIES (LO 2 & 3)

This section will discuss accounting issues that are unique to partnerships. There is a special relationship between a partner and a partnership that causes accounting for investments in and distributions from a partnership to be different than for a corporation. This special relationship also causes a unique definition of partnership income and special procedures associated with the allocation of profit or loss to the individual partners.

Forming a Partnership (LO 2)

Leo and April form a general partnership, *A&L CPAs*. The basic accounting issues are the same regardless of whether they choose a partnership or an LLP. Leo purchased his computer system for $5,000. April acquired her computer system for $10,000. The acquisition cost approximates the fair value of these assets.

An advantage of a partnership is that the individuals can decide how they want to form and structure their operation. Therefore, they decided to each contribute their computer system. They recognized the need for operating capital. April will contribute $10,000, and Leo will contribute $5,000. Therefore, the initial capital contribution for both partners is:

April $20,000
Leo $10,000

These balances consist of each individual partner's cash contribution as well as the contribution of non-cash assets. **Non-cash assets** contributed are valued using the asset's fair market value at the time the asset is contributed to the partnership. Contributions to the partnership increase the partner's capital interest or his/her **basis** in the partnership. These assets are now the property of the partnership.

Liabilities can also be associated with an asset contributed to the partnership. For example, there are two partners, A and B. Partner A contributes a building with a fair market value of $100,000, then partner A's capital interest is $100,000. Also, there is a $30,000 mortgage associated with the building partner A contributed. The partnership can assume responsibility for the mortgage. When this happens, the basis of the contributing partner is decreased based upon the amount of liability assumed by the other partners.

Continuing the above example: If the partnership assumes the liability, then partner A's capital interest is only $70,000. There may be complicating issues associated with the partner's **tax basis**. It is possible that a partner will have a capital interest in the accounting records that is different from his/her tax basis. For instance, if partner A originally acquired the building discussed above for $80,000, then A's tax basis is $80,000 less the $30,000 mortgage, or $50,000. The different values between the partner and the partnership create a separate basis for each taxpayer. The partner maintains her **original basis** without recognizing any gain ($50,000), and the partnership has a **stepped-up basis** based upon the asset's fair market value at the time it is contributed ($100,000). The tax implications to the partners associated with contributing appreciated assets will be discussed in more detail in Chapter 3.

● INTERPRETIVE EXERCISE

Based upon the above description, what are the assets found on the *A&L* partnership balance sheet? What do you find different about how assets are valued and classified for a partnership versus a corporation?

Additional Investments and Withdrawals

The partnership agreement allows the partners the ability to decide how partners can contribute additional capital in the business and also how funds can be distributed from the partnership to the partners. Funds can flow from partners to the partnership in the form of additional capital contributions or in the form of loans to the business. When a partner loans money to the partnership, there should be a methodology for preparing a note and assuring a proper rate of interest on the loan. The same holds true should the partnership loan funds to a partner. There then needs to be a method to establish the receivable and to charge the partner an appropriate rate of interest.

The partnership must account for all disbursements or distributions to the individual partners. The partners are assumed to receive the profits from operating the business. They are not considered to be employees, and, therefore, partners are not paid what is considered to be a usual salary for the normal duties associated with operating the partnership. However, they are allowed to take an advance or withdrawal against the profits of the partnership. A separate **drawing account** is established to account for the withdrawals for each partner. These drawing accounts are closed to the individual partner's account at the end of the year. Accounting for the partner's capital or equity is a significant difference in comparing a partnership to a corporation (Table 1-1).

TABLE 1-1 Accounting for Equity: Partnership vs Corporation

	Partnership	Corporation
Ownership	Partner's Capital Account	Common Stock
Income earned by the entity	Increase Partner's Capital Account	Retained Earnings
Return to Owner Distributions	Decrease Capital Account, Partner's Drawing Account is closed to the Partner's Capital Account at the end of the year	Dividends, decrease Retained Earnings

In T-account format, the following occurs:

Drawing Account	
Periodic withdrawal of partnership asset	Annual closing of Drawing Account

Partnership Capital	
Annual Closing of Drawing Account	Beginning Balance
	Contributions
Allocation of Net Loss	Allocation of Net Income
	Ending Balance

Partnership Operations

Accounting for partnership operations is basically the same as that for any other form of organization. Revenues and expenses, including depreciation, will be recorded. A partnership associated with the manufacture or distribution of goods needs to account for inventory and the cost of goods sold. A form of operation that is significantly product oriented is accounted for using the accrual basis.

April and Leo have contributed computers to the partnership. These assets will be assumed to have a useful life of 5 years. The depreciation expense for the partnership will be computed using straight-line depreciation. Total depreciation expense for *A&L* will be $3,000 per year.

Allocation of Net Income or Net Loss (LO 3)

As stated above, partners are not considered to be employees and are not paid a salary. Usually, the partners make withdrawals from the partnership in anticipation of profits. Some of these withdrawals may be referred to as salary because the withdrawals occur periodically; however, this salary withdrawal is not subject to payroll taxes and income tax withholding requirements. In establishing the partnership, the partners need to decide how the net income or net loss from operations will be allocated among the partners. As stated previously, the income or loss is divided equally among the partners unless the partnership agreement provides for a different arrangement. The following paragraphs will discuss alternatives that may be included in the partnership agreement to aid the partners in defining what they assume will be an equitable allocation of partnership earnings.

April and Leo wanted to plan for the **allocation of net income**. They discussed a variety of issues, including whether to pay each partner a salary. Their opinion was that they would be able to attract sufficient clients to support a monthly salary of $3,000 each. Partners are not obligated to withdraw their salary. Even if the partners withdraw a salary, the partnership does not deduct payroll taxes. For tax purposes, the partnership agreement should state the amount of salary each partner is entitled to receive and whether or not this is a guaranteed right of the partner regardless of overall partnership profitability. This issue of guaranteed payments is covered further in Chapter 3.

Many accountants define partnership income as the income earned prior to deducting "partner's salary." Under this theory, "partner's salary" is treated as a method of helping to equitably divide or allocate partnership earnings.

Another issue bothering April was that she had always received a hefty **bonus** for putting in extra hours during the tax season. Leo's work in assurance services had been spread out smoothly throughout the year, and he was not as dependent upon the bonus as April. They decided that if either one of them worked more hours than the other, then the bonus would be a percentage of the extra hours. The bonus would be based upon the partnership profits after salary and the bonus.

This bonus would be computed based upon the following: If April works 2,200 hours and Leo works 2,000 hours, then April is entitled to a 10% bonus (2,200 – 2000 = 200/2000 = 10%). Assume that first year net income is $105,000 prior to salaries ($36,000 each or $72,000 in total) and bonus. As calculated below, April's bonus would be $3,000. See Figure 1-1 for examples of other potential types of bonus computations.

$$\text{Bonus} = 10\% \ (\text{Profits} - \text{Salaries} - \text{Bonus})$$
$$\text{Bonus} = 10\% \ (105,000 - 72,000 - \text{Bonus})$$
$$\text{Bonus} = 10\% \ (33,000 - B)$$
$$1.1\text{Bonus} = 3,300$$
$$\text{Bonus} = \$3,000$$

FIGURE 1-1 Methods for Computing a Partner's Bonus

Partners can agree on how to allocate profits. Computing bonuses is one way to equitably compensate individual partners. The calculation chosen by April and Leo allows them to accomplish their individual goals. Other typical bonus computations include:

Bonus as a Percentage of Income before the Bonus:
Assume the partnership agreement allows for April to receive a 10% bonus prior to payment of salaries.
   The bonus would be calculated as:

$$\text{Bonus} = 10\% \ \text{Income before Salaries}$$
$$\text{Bonus} = 10\% \ (\$105,000)$$
$$\text{Bonus} = \$10,500$$

Bonus as a Percentage of Income after the Bonus:
Assume the partnership agreement allows for April to receive a 10% bonus prior to payment of salaries but after paying the bonus.
   The bonus would be calculated as:

$$\text{Bonus} = 10\%(\text{Income} - \text{Bonus}) \qquad\qquad \text{Bonus} = 10\%(\$105,000 - B)$$
$$\text{Bonus} = 10\% \ \text{Income} - 10\% \ \text{Bonus} \qquad\qquad \text{Bonus} = 10,500 - (.1B)$$
$$1.1 \ \text{Bonus} = .1 \text{Income} \qquad\qquad\qquad 1.1 \ \text{Bonus} = 10,500$$
$$\text{Bonus} = \frac{.1 \text{Income}}{1.1} \qquad\qquad\qquad\qquad \text{Bonus} = \frac{10,500}{1.1}$$
$$\text{Bonus} = \$9,545$$

April was also concerned that her original capital contribution was larger than Leo's. Leo suggested that they both could be paid an **interest allowance on their capital balances**. They decided to pay each partner 10% of the beginning capital balance. They could have chosen other methods, such as, their ending balance or their weighted-average balance. See Figure 1-2 for example computations of other methods used to compute interest on capital balances.

This would result in the following allocation:

April Beginning Capital Balance: $20,000 * 10% = $2,000
Leo Beginning Capital Balance: $10,000 * 10% = $1,000

FIGURE 1-2 Alternative Methods for Computing Interest Allowance on a Partner's Capital Balance

Providing an interest allowance is one way to equitably compensate individual partners as they allocate profits and losses. Alternative methods include those using ending balances before allocating current-year income or using a weighted average of the capital balances during the year.

Assume there are two partners, A and B, with the following transactions impacting their capital accounts during the year.

	A	B
Beginning Balance	$10,000	$20,000
Contributions:		
Feb. 28	10,000	10,000
June 1		10,000
Nov. 1	10,000	
Withdrawals:		
Aug 1	5,000	
Ending balance	$25,000	$40,000

Ending Balance before allocating current-year income:
The partners agree to pay each other 6% on their ending capital balances:

	A	B
Ending Balance	$25,000	$40,000
Interest percentage	6%	6%
Interest on the Capital Balance	$ 1,500	$ 2,400

Weighted-Average Method:
The partners agree to pay each other 6% on their weighted-average capital balances during the year.

Weighted-Average Schedule for Partner A			Weighted-Average Schedule for Partner B		
Amount Invested	Number of Months	Weighted Dollars	Amount Invested	Number of Months	Weighted Dollars
$10,000	2	20,000	$ 20,000	2	40,000
20,000	5	100,000	30,000	3	90,000
15,000	3	45,000	40,000	7	280,000
25,000	2	50,000			
	12	215,000		12	410,000

Weighted-Average Capital = $215,000/12 = $17,917 $410,000/12 = $34,167

	A	B
Weighted-Average Capital Balance	$17,917	$34,167
Interest percentage	6%	6%
Interest on the Capital Balance	$ 1,075	$ 2,050

They finally decide that the remaining profit and loss would be split equally between each other. Assuming the partnership had Net Income of $105,000 prior to paying salaries, bonus, and interest on the capital balance, then the first-year Allocation of Net Income would be as depicted in Figure 1-3:

FIGURE 1-3 Allocation of A&L First-year Net Income

	April	Leo	Total Allocated
Salary ($3,000/month)	$ 36,000	$36,000	$ 72,000
Bonus	$ 3,000		$ 3,000
Interest on the Capital Balance	$ 2,000	$ 1,000	$ 3,000
Subtotal	$ 41,000	$37,000	$ 78,000
Remaining Profit	$ 13,500	$13,500	$ 27,000
Income Allocation	$ 54,500	$50,500	$105,000

The partners were able to write the partnership agreement to meet their needs. This flexibility is an advantage with a partnership. As a result, for income tax purposes April will report $54,500 and Leo will report $50,500. Both are now subject to self-employment tax.

Both partners withdrew their salary during the year. At the end of December, April and Leo made additional capital contributions of $1,600 and $500, respectively. The bonus was not known until the end of the year, so April did not withdraw any amount associated with the bonus prior to year-end. The year-end capital accounts would appear as follows:

	April, Capital		Leo, Capital	
Initial Contribution		20,000		10,000
Capital Contribution		1,600		500
Close Drawing	36,000		36,000	
Allocation of Income		54,400		50,500
Ending Balance		40,000		25,000

● **INTERPRETIVE QUESTION**

Assume that April's and Leo's partnership agreement did not require payments for either bonus or interest on capital. Instead, they decide to have profit or loss ratio of 60% for April and 40% for Leo. What would the income allocation be for each partner? What is their ending Capital Balance? Explain why this income allocation process is reasonable for *A&L CPAs*.

This question is to aid in understanding the material. April's and Leo's original partnership agreement was not modified in the narrative.

Insufficient Income to Cover Allowable Allocations

Assume that April and Leo have first-year net income of $74,200 rather than $105,000 and they have the same allocation of profit or loss methodology described above. The Income/Loss Allocation would look like Figure 1-4:

FIGURE 1-4 Allocation of A&L First-year Net Income: Assuming Insufficient Income

	April	Leo	Total Allocated
Salary ($3,000/month)	$36,000	$36,000	$72,000
Bonus	$ 200		$ 200
Interest on the Capital Balance	$ 2,000	$ 1,000	$ 3,000
Subtotal	$38,200	$37,000	$75,200
Remaining Profit	$ (500)	$ (500)	$ (1,000)
Income Allocation	$37,700	$36,500	$74,200

There was no change in the computation of interest on the capital balance. The bonus was computed based upon the following:

$$\text{Bonus} = 10\% \ ((74,200 - 72,000) - (\text{Bonus})) = 2,200/1.1 = \$200.$$

April's and Leo's partnership agreement required the bonus and the interest on the capital balance. Therefore, a deficit was computed because there was not sufficient income to provide for the salaries, the bonus, and the interest on the capital balance. The partners share this deficit based upon their profit and loss ratio, which in this situation means the partners will share equally.

The overriding document is the partnership agreement. By agreeing originally to the partnership agreement, April and Leo have determined for themselves an equitable allocation of the partnership income.

WHAT MAKES A PARTNER COMPENSATION PLAN EFFECTIVE?

In the January 1998 issue of *The CPA Journal*, Marc Rosenberg discusses 14 different compensation strategies that can be used by partners. He emphasizes that "a fair and motivating partner compensation system isn't the only important thing, but it goes a long way." (page 50). While all partnerships may not be able to implement all 14 items, implementing as many as possible helps. Some examples of the strategies include:

- The best systems are performance-based.
- The system should motivate the partners to do what the firm needs them to do.
- The system should reward the values the partners feel are most important.
- Most partners must perceive the system as fair.
- The system should be flexible.
- Marketing should play a meaningful role.
- Compensation systems should be integrated with goal setting and performance evaluation of partners.

"Not All Partners Are Created Equal," Marc L. Rosenberg, *The CPA Journal*, January 1998, pp. 46–50.

CHANGES IN PARTNERSHIP INTEREST (LO 4)

An advantage of a partnership is that individuals can agree to form an organization; a disadvantage is that ownership does not easily change hands. A corporation can issue shares of stock to obtain new investors. Stockholders wanting to divest their ownership interest in a publicly held corporation can sell shares to a willing buyer on the open market. On the other hand, a partnership is assumed to cease when an owner leaves or a new partner is added. Partnerships can plan for partners joining or leaving the organization in the partnership agreement.

An individual partner has the right to sell or assign his or her interest in the partnership. The other partners, however, do not have to admit the buyer as a partner. The buyer does have contractual rights to receive the profits of the selling partner. For example A, B, and C are all partners. A can sell her income rights of the partnership to D. B and C do not have to allow D to be involved in managing the partnership. However, at the end of the year the profits due A would be paid to D. The other examples used throughout the narrative assume that the partners agree with the admission of the new partner.

◢ CONCEPTUAL QUESTION AND REFLECTION

Why would a partner consider assigning a partnership interest to a third party that would not be allowed to participate in the management of the partnership? Why would a third party accept such an interest?

Let's return to April and Leo, who have capital balances of $40,000 and $25,000, respectively. They have been providing tax and assurance services but realize they don't have the expertise to provide a client a forensic accounting engagement. They face a choice about the future of their partnership. April's college classmate, Sheri, who works for a different firm in the same city, has developed the needed experience. April contacts Sheri about joining *A&L*.

Valuation Issues

In admitting a new partner, the existing partners have to agree to the method used in valuing the new partner's interest in the existing partnership. When addressing this issue in drafting the partnership agreement, there are a variety of issues to be considered:

1. Does the new partner need to purchase an equity interest in the partnership?
2. If the new partner does not need to purchase an interest, will the partnership interest be based upon future service?
3. If a partner does need to purchase an equity interest, how should this interest be valued:
   a. book value;
   b. more than book value; or
   c. less than book value?
4. What profit and loss interest will the new partner have after admission?

SELLING A PARTNERSHIP INTEREST OUTSIDE OF THE PARTNERSHIP April and/or Leo could each sell a portion of their profit and loss interest in the partnership. In this situation, the transaction occurs outside of the partnership. For instance, if Sheri should purchase a 10% interest from April for $5,000, the transaction would appear as follows in the partnership records:

April, Capital $4,000
            Sheri, Capital $4,000

April's capital of $4,000 ($40,000 * 10% = $4,000) is transferred to Sheri. Total partnership capital does not change and is still $65,000. The $5,000 was transferred outside of the partnership and does not result in an entry on the partnership books. The new partner's capital represents an acquired profit interest in the partnership.

The new partner's capital balance represents an acquired profit interest in the partnership. Should the new partner be acquiring a profit interest from more than one partner, then the capital balance allocation is based upon the profit and loss sharing ratio of each partner involved in the transaction.

ADMITTING A NEW PARTNER AT BOOK VALUE April and Leo recognize a need for more operating capital and expect the new partner to contribute equity to the partnership. If they were to allow Sheri to acquire a 20% interest while contributing based upon the partnership's *book value*, the transaction would appear as such in the partnership records:

Partnership net book value ($40,000 + $25,000) $65,000 * 20% = $13,000

Cash   13,000
            Sheri, Capital   13,000

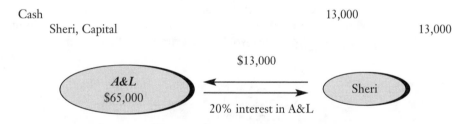

This transaction can be seen as occurring between the partnership and Sheri. Therefore, the net assets in the partnership have increased to $78,000. When Sheri has been admitted, the new partner profit interests will be:

April   40%
Leo   40%
Sheri   20%

The profit interests were reallocated based upon the partners' original profit interests. Since each partner began with a 50% interest, they each allocated 10% (50% * 20%) of their profit interest to Sheri.

ADMITTING A NEW PARTNER WITH BONUS OR GOODWILL TRACEABLE TO THE EXISTING PARTNERS April and Leo decide to offer Sheri a 20% interest in the partnership for $20,000. In this case, Sheri is contributing to the partnership an amount in excess of the book value. She might want to do this because the existing partnership offers her a variety of opportunities and she is rewarding the existing partners for developing the organization. Or, she may be of the opinion that the existing partnership assets, tangible and intangible, are undervalued and she is contributing based upon their fair market value. These different reasons for paying in excess of book value, i.e., a premium, are supported by two different methodologies: the **bonus method** and the **goodwill method**.

BONUS METHOD The **bonus method** assumes existing partners to be the owners of the partnership. The contribution of any amount in excess of the partnership's net book value can then be considered as a bonus to the individual partners. The bonus method attempts to be consistent with GAAP by being conservative and not increasing asset values. This method does recognize that the asset values could be overstated and recognizes a decrease in book value for assets with an impaired value. In this manner, any increases in the capital of existing partners can be considered to be the result of a decrease in the capital of the incoming partner.

$$\frac{\text{New Partner's}}{\text{Capital Balance}} = \left(\frac{\text{Existing Partnership}}{\text{Net Book Value}} - \text{Impaired Assets} + \frac{\text{New Partner's}}{\text{Contribution}} \right) * \frac{\text{New Partner's}}{\text{Equity \%}}$$

For example, a partnership has $80,000 of net assets, including a piece of equipment that is overvalued by $10,000. A new partner is contributing $20,000 for a 20% interest.

New Balance = (($80,000 – $10,000) + $20,000) * 20%) = $18,000. So there is a $2,000 bonus to be split by the existing partners.

April and Leo don't have any impaired assets. Therefore, the computation of Sheri's equity interest is:

(($65,000 – 0) + $20,000) * 20% = $17,000, which implies a $3,000 bonus to April and Leo. This would be recorded by the partnership as:

Cash	20,000	
April, Capital		1,500
Leo, Capital		1,500
Sheri, Capital		17,000

April and Leo are sharing the bonus based upon their original profit interest (50% each). This example assumes Sheri contributed cash. She could have contributed any asset(s), which would be valued based upon the fair market value of the asset(s). A schedule supporting the computation could be constructed as:

Capital Interest Acquired	$17,000
Capital Contribution	$20,000
Bonus to Existing Partners	$ (3,000)

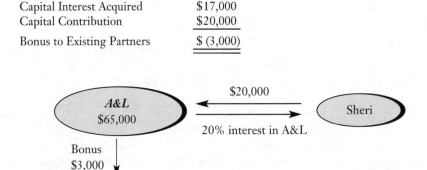

Partner Characteristics after admitting Sheri to the Partnership:

	April	Leo	Sheri	Total
Capital Balances	$41,500	$26,500	$17,000	$85,000
Profit Interests	40%	40%	20%	

GOODWILL METHOD The **goodwill method** assumes that the assets of the existing partnership will be revalued to fair market value. This is consistent with the assumption that admitting a new partner represents the end of the previous entity and the beginning of a new economic entity. Procedurally, this method uses the agreed-upon fair market value of the asset(s) contributed and the resulting new partner's profit interest to value the partnership. As shown in Figure 1-5, any existing undervalued (overvalued) assets should be written up (down) to fair market value.

FIGURE 1-5 Goodwill Method Including Impact of Over/Undervalued Tangible and Intangible Assets

To properly implement the goodwill method, the partnership must evaluate all existing tangible and intangible assets. This provides for a proper valuation of the new entity as it goes forward. For example, assume that C is contributing $40,000 for a 10% interest in the XYZ partnership. This partnership has an existing book value of $250,000 with the following information about the assets:

	Asset Description		
	Book Value	**Fair Market Value**	**Difference**
Cash	$ 30,000	$ 30,000	
Accounts Receivable	$ 45,000	$ 45,000	
Inventory	$ 85,000	$ 85,000	
Building	$ 60,000	$100,000	$40,000
Equipment	$ 30,000	$ 20,000	($10,000)
Patent	$ 0	$ 15,000	$15,000
	$250,000	$295,000	

The goodwill method valuation of the XYZ Partnership would be:

Contribution/Interest = Implied Fair Market Value:

   $40,000/10% = $400,000

This computation of fair market value is then used to compute the goodwill to be allocated to the partners:

Implied Fair Market Value of the partnership		$ 400,000
Less: Original Book Value		$(250,000)
Excess		$ 150,000
Less: Unrecognized asset value (undervalued assets):		
Building	$40,000	
Patent	$15,000	
		$ (55,000)
Plus: Overvalued assets (impaired assets) Equipment	$10,000	
Less: Fair Market Value of Assets Contributed		$ (40,000)
Goodwill to be allocated to Existing Partners		$ 65,000

(continued on next page)

Another way of viewing this is that the new valuation of the partnership is based upon:

Existing XYZ Partnership net asset value:		$250,000
Plus: Unrecognized asset value (undervalued assets):		
Building	$40,000	
Patent	$15,000	
		$ 55,000
Less: Overvalued assets (impaired assets)		$ (10,000)
Plus: Fair Market Value of Assets Contributed		$ 40,000
Plus: Unrecorded Intangible Assets: Goodwill		$ 65,000
Fair Market Value of XYZ Partnership		$400,000

The journal entry to record the change in asset values would include:

Building	40,000	
Patent	15,000	
Equipment		10,000
Existing Partner, Capital		45,000

The journal entry to record the goodwill would include:

Goodwill	65,000	
Existing Partner, Capital		65,000

The journal entry to record C's contribution would include:

Cash	40,000	
C, Capital		40,000

Let's compute the valuation of April's and Leo's partnership using the goodwill method based upon Sheri accepting their offer to join the partnership by contributing $20,000 for a 20% profit interest. The implied fair market value of the partnership is $100,000.

Implied fair market value: ($20,000/20%) =		$100,000
April's + Leo's Capital	$65,000	
Sheri's Contribution	$20,000	
New Partnership Capital		$ 85,000
Partnership Goodwill not recorded		$ 15,000

There are no over/undervalued assets, and there are no other unrecorded intangible assets. GAAP has provisions for valuing some specific asset categories, such as investments at market. However, GAAP does not provide procedures for updating the historical cost of fixed assets of a continuing economic entity. The revaluation of continuing partnerships has been an acceptable accounting procedure that assumes that the legal concept of beginning a new organization has been fulfilled. This process then becomes consistent with the GAAP definition of goodwill in that it must be purchased and not self-constructed.

The entry to record this transaction on the partnership books, assuming the contributed asset is cash:

Cash	20,000	
Goodwill	15,000	
April, Capital		7,500
Leo, Capital		7,500
Sheri, Capital		20,000

April's and Leo's capital accounts increased based upon their profit interest percentages prior to Sheri joining. Although there is not a bonus recorded by April and Leo, their individual capital accounts are increased to reflect the new partnership valuation.

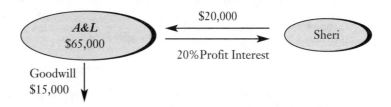

Partner Characteristics after admitting Sheri to the Partnership:

	April	**Leo**	**Sheri**	**Total**
Capital Balances	$47,500	$32,500	$20,000	$100,000
Profit Interests	40%	40%	20%	

"PARTNERS THAT WORK WELL TOGETHER PROFIT FROM EACH OTHER"

Marc Rosenberg discusses this fundamental notion in an article in *Accounting Today*. Partners need to clearly establish their responsibilities up front if they want to eventually hold individual partners accountable. Partners need to understand their responsibility:

- to obtain new clients,
- to bill and collect for work performed,
- to properly treat associates, and
- to be role models for other firm behaviors.

In order to maintain good working relationships and to have a profitable partnership, the partners need to learn to communicate effectively with each other. "Show me a firm that has a partner group that communicates well with each other, and I'll show you a profitable firm because each partner knows, accepts and performs his or her role in the firm and sensitive issues are addressed instead of swept under the carpet." He also emphasizes: "Communication is easier to describe than to define, but most of us recognize good communication when we see it. It may seem like a cliché, but good communication is vital to a firm's success."

Notice that your ultimate success can depend on strong interpersonal and communication skills. Practice these skills on a regular basis.

"Practice Management Forum: When Partnerships Go Sour," Marc Rosenberg, *Accounting Today*, July 28 – Aug 8, 1999, pp. 9, 48+.

ADMITTING A NEW PARTNER WITH THE BONUS OR GOODWILL TRACEABLE TO THE NEW PARTNER April and Leo decide to offer Sheri a 20% interest in the partnership for $12,000. In this case, Sheri is contributing to the partnership an amount that is less than the book value. April and Leo might want to do this because they believe Sheri has much to offer the partnership, either in contributed assets or professional potential, and they want to entice her to join **A&L**. Also, it is possible that the existing assets are overvalued or impaired and need to be written down.

BONUS METHOD The bonus method values the partnership based upon the book value of the net assets. Again, for **A&L** there are no tangible or intangible assets that need to be revalued. The computation of the new partner's balance is:

$$\begin{array}{l}\text{New Partner's} \\ \text{Capital Balance}\end{array} = \left(\begin{array}{l}\text{Existing Partnership} \\ \text{Net Book Value}\end{array} - \text{Impaired Assets} + \begin{array}{l}\text{New Partner's} \\ \text{Contribution}\end{array} \right) * \begin{array}{l}\text{New Partner's} \\ \text{Equity \%}\end{array}$$

$$\$15,400 = (\$65,000 - 0 + \$12,000) * 20\%$$

In this case, Sheri's Capital Balance is greater than the fair value of the assets contributed. Therefore, the existing partners are paying her a bonus of $3,400 to join the partnership. This would be recorded by the partnership with this journal entry:

Cash	12,000	
April, Capital	1,700	
Leo, Capital	1,700	
Sheri, Capital		15,400

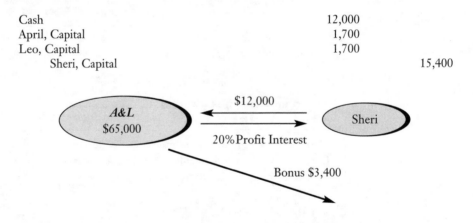

Partner Characteristics after admitting Sheri to the Partnership:

	April	Leo	Sheri	Total
Capital Balances	$38,300	$23,300	$15,400	$77,000
Profit Interests	40%	40%	20%	

A&L did not have any impaired assets. If there were impaired assets, they would be written down first. Then the remainder of the difference would reduce the existing partners' capital balances based upon their profit interests prior to admitting the new partner. For instance, assume a partnership with $100,000 of assets is admitting a new partner with a 20% capital interest for $10,000. The partnership has overstated assets of $20,000. In this situation, the new partner's balance is $18,000 ((100,000 − 20,000) + 10,000) * 20%. The entries will be:

Existing Partners, Capital	20,000	
Assets		20,000

Cash	10,000	
Existing Partners, Capital	8,000	
New Partner, Capital		18,000

GOODWILL METHOD The partnership will be revalued to its fair market value. In doing this it will be noted that the implied fair market value is less than the book value.

Implied fair market value = ($12,000/20%) = $60,000 < $65,000 Book value.

If this situation is discovered, then the schedule prepared earlier results in a negative goodwill.

Implied fair market value		$ 60,000
Existing capital	$65,000	
New contribution	12,000	
Revised book value		77,000
Negative goodwill		($17,000)

Therefore, in this situation, the following computation is employed:

$$\frac{\text{New Partner}}{\text{Capital Balance}} = \left(\frac{\text{(Existing Partnership Book Value)}}{\text{Remaining Ownership \%}} - \text{Existing Patnership Book Value} \right)$$

$$\$16,250 = ((\$65,000/\mathbf{80\%}) - \$65,000) = (81,250 - 65,000)$$

This results in Sheri having a capital balance of $16,250 with a contribution of assets of $12,000. This creates goodwill associated with her admission to the partnership of $4,250. This transaction could be recorded by the partnership as:

Cash	12,000	
Goodwill	4,250	
Sheri, Capital		16,250

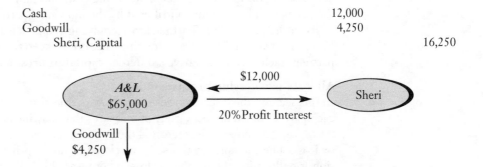

Partner Characteristics after admitting Sheri to the Partnership:

	April	Leo	Sheri	Total
Capital Balances	$40,000	$25,000	$16,250	$81,250
Profit Interests	40%	40%	20%	

Should impaired tangible or intangible assets exist, then the existing partners' capital balance would be decreased along with these assets. Then the partnership would compute the goodwill associated with adding the new partner. *A&L* did not have any impaired tangible or intangible assets.

● **INTERPRETIVE EXERCISE**

April and Leo decide to offer Sheri a 20% interest in the partnership for $15,000. Who receives the bonus or goodwill (April & Leo, or Sheri)? What is the partnership valuation using: bonus method? goodwill method? Explain how you know which method is being used.

SUMMARY

In this chapter, there were four **Learning Objectives**:

- Discuss the legal issues associated with forming and operating a partnership.
- Determine a partner's capital balance when forming a partnership.
- Allocate partnership profits and losses.
- Compute a partner's capital balance when a partnership's ownership changes.

Discuss the legal issues associated with forming and operating a partnership.
Associated with this learning objective, the discussion included defining a partnership as an association of two or more individuals or entities that are in a legal profit-making operation. A partnership operates under the **UPA** unless a separate **partnership agreement** has been established. A partnership is distinguished from a corporation relative to some legal advantages and disadvantages such as **mutual agency**, **unlimited liability**, **limited life**, and **no income taxes** paid by the partnership.

Determine a partner's capital balance when forming a partnership.
In this section, April and Leo formed a **general partnership**. The partnership was valued based upon the fair market value of the cash and non-cash assets contributed by the partners. The amount contributed by the individual partner determines his or her **basis** in the partnership. Partnership accounting requires a separate **capital account** for each partner and a separate **drawing account** to keep track of distributions to each partner. Each partner can have a different **capital interest** and **profit interest**.

Allocate partnership profits and loss.
In this section, the discussion related to how partnership earnings may be allocated to each partner based upon a variety of measures that may include salary, bonus, or interest on capital. The profit interest is then used to allocate the remaining Net Income or Loss. The examples in this section related to how April and Leo made their decision for allocating the income or loss. There was also a discussion of different methods for computing a partner's bonus, as well as alternative methods for computing the interest allowance on a partner's capital balance.

Compute a partner's capital balance when a partnership's ownership changes.
This last section discussed the addition of a partner. Sheri was added to the *A&L* partnership. A variety of valuation issues were discussed that related to admitting a new partner at book value, greater than book value, or less than book value. For situations when the partner contributes at other than book value, the partnership needs to decide upon the use of the **bonus method** or **goodwill method**.

The Bonus Method attempts to be consistent with GAAP. This accounting method tends to be conservative by not increasing asset values. The Goodwill Method assumes the beginning of a new entity and revalues partnership assets to fair market value.

WHAT COMES NEXT?

Chapter 1 discussed the formation of a partnership and the addition of a new partner. Chapter 2 will explore the situations when a partner wants to retire or leave a partnership or when the business ends and the partnership must be liquidated.

Chapter 1 ignores the income tax implications of the partnership transactions. An advantage of a partnership is that it is a pass-through entity and the partnership does not pay an entity-level income tax. However, the partners are responsible for paying income tax. Chapter 3 discusses many of the associated tax issues.

QUESTIONS

1. Define a partnership.
2. Contrast and compare at least two advantages and two disadvantages of a partnership form of organization with a corporate form of organization.
3. Explain the differences between a profit interest and a capital interest.
4. What is meant by a "partner's basis" in a partnership?
5. A and B form a partnership. A contributes cash and B contributes marketable securities. How is B's capital balance determined?
6. Compare the equity section of a partnership's balance sheet with the equity section of a corporation's balance sheet.
7. Describe the differences between the Cash Basis of Accounting and the Accrual Basis of Accounting.
8. Partners A and B decide on a profit ratio such that A gets $3 for every $5 B gets. Explain what this means.
9. Explain why partnerships consider offering partners "interest on capital" in addition to paying salaries and bonuses. Provide an example of why this might occur.
10. E and F are looking to have G join their partnership. What are the options available to E and F regarding G?
11. XYZ has given A an offer to join their partnership by contributing $20,000 for a 20% interest in their partnership when XYZ has a book value of $80,000. Would you recommend to A to contribute an amount to the partnership in excess of book value?
12. MNOP is a partnership with a book value of $120,000. They are short of cash. Why might the partners propose that B joins the partnership by contributing $30,000 for a 30% interest?
13. Partnerships are allowed to ignore GAAP in accounting for their operations. How are the bonus method and the goodwill method supported by GAAP concepts?

EXERCISES

Exercise 1-1

Multiple Choice—Select the best answer for each of the following.

1. Which of the following is an advantage of a partnership?
    a. limited liability
    b. limited life
    c. mutual agency
    d. double taxation

2. Mutual Agency allows
   a. partners to work together.
   b. other businesses to conduct business with individual partners.
   c. partners to conduct business with partnerships.
   d. the partnership to conduct business with corporations.

3. John contributes the following to A&B partnership:

Cash	$ 20,000
Securities FMV	$ 30,000 cost $15,000
Building FMV	$100,000 mortgage of $30,000 not assumed by the partnership

   What is John's capital balance after the contributions?
   a. $150,000
   b. $135,000
   c. $120,000
   d. $105,000

4. Paul has a 40% profit interest in J&P partnership. He began the year with a $20,000 capital balance. During the year, the partnership earned $60,000 and Paul received distributions of :

Cash	$5,000
Equipment	$6,000

   What is Paul's capital balance at the end of the year?
   a. $91,000
   b. $69,999
   c. $55,000
   d. $33,000

5. A&B partnership uses the cash basis of accounting. Assume the following are all the transactions that occurred during the period.

Cash sales	$50,000
Credit sales	$80,000
Collection from customers	$60,000
Interest paid	$10,000
Increase in interest payable	$ 5,000

   What is income using the cash basis?
   a. $180,000
   b. $175,000
   c. $100,000
   d. $95,000

6. X&Y partnership has net income of $100,000. Y is to receive a bonus equal to 20% of Net Income after the bonus. How much is Y's bonus?
   a. $83,333
   b. $20,000
   c. $16,667
   d. $10,000

7. A and B share equally in their partnership. A&B's current capital balances are $60,000 and $40,000, respectively. C contributes $25,000 for a 20% interest. Using the bonus method, what is A's new capital balance?
   a. $72,500
   b. $62,500
   c. $60,000
   d. $57,500

8. E and F share equally in their partnership. E's and F's current capital balances are $55,000 and $45,000, respectively. G contributes $18,000 for a 15% interest. Using the goodwill method, what is E's new capital balance?
   a. $65,000
   b. $57,000
   c. $56,000
   d. $55,000

9. X and Y share equally in their partnership. X's and Y's current capital balances are $65,000 and $45,000. Z contributes $20,000 for a 20% interest when the partnership owns equipment with a $40,000 book value that has a $30,000 fair market value. Using the bonus method, what is Z's capital balance?
   a. $26,400
   b. $24,000
   c. $22,000
   d. $20,000

10. X and Y share equally in their partnership. X's and Y's current capital balances are $65,000 and $45,000. Z contributes $20,000 for a 20% interest when the partnership owns equipment with a $40,000 book value that has a $30,000 fair market value. Using the goodwill method, what is Z's capital balance?
    a. $20,000
    b. $22,000
    c. $24,000
    d. $26,400

Exercise 1-2

Form a Partnership with Cash (LO 2)

Peter and Mary decide to form a partnership. Peter contributes $40,000, and Mary contributes $20,000. They will share profits and losses equally.
   a. What is the amount of the partnership's total assets?
   b. What is the profit-sharing ratio for each partner?
   c. Compute Peter's capital balance immediately upon forming the partnership.

Exercise 1-3

Form a Partnership with Assets (LO 2)

On 6/1/x2, Johnson and Lever form a partnership where they agree to a 60/40 profit-sharing ratio. Johnson contributes land that cost him $20,000. Lever contributes $30,000 cash. Immediately upon forming the partnership on June 1, the property was sold for $25,000.
   a. What is Johnson's capital balance immediately upon forming the partnership?
   b. What is the amount of the partnership's total assets?

Exercise 1-4

Partner Contributions and Withdrawals (LO 2)

On 1/1/x2, Tony and Ken form a partnership with Tony contributing $30,000 and Ken contributing $35,000. During the year, the partnership earned $50,000 and the following transactions occurred between the partners and the partnership:

February 1, Tony contributes $10,000.
April 1, each partner withdraws $15,000.
September 1, Tony withdraws $5,000.

   a. Compute the 12/31/x2 capital balance for each partner if the profit-sharing ratio is 50/50.
   b. Compute the 12/31/x2 capital balance for each partner if the profit-sharing ratio is 70/30.

Exercise 1-5

Compute Partner Bonus (LO 3)

Mary closes more customers than Peter. They decide that Mary will receive a 20% bonus on the partnership income after paying the bonus. Compute Mary's bonus if the partnership earns $100,000.

Exercise 1-6

Compute Interest on Partner Weighted-Average Capital Balance (LO 3)

Peter and Mary begin their partnership on 1/1/x2 by contributing $40,000 and $20,000, respectively. They agree to pay each partner 8% interest on the weighted-average capital balance. Compute the interest on the capital balances for both partners assuming the following transactions occurred during 20x2:

February 1, Mary contributed $5,000
April 1, both partners withdrew $5,000
August 1, Peter contributed $10,000
November 1, both partners withdrew $5,000

Exercise 1-7

Allocate Income: Continuation of Exercises 5 & 6 (LO 3)

Peter and Mary are sharing profits equally. Based upon Exercises 5 and 6, what is the ending capital balance for each partner if the partnership earns $100,000 before Mary's bonus? Assume Bonus and Interest are paid in the year after they are earned.

Exercise 1-8

Allocate Income: Partners Have Different Income-Sharing Ratio (LO 3)

Johnson and Lever share profits and losses 60/40. Johnson receives a salary of $20,000, and Lever receives a salary of $15,000. Each partner receives 6% interest on his or her beginning capital balances of $30,000 and $25,000, respectively. How is the net income divided if the partnership earns $100,000?

Exercise 1-9

Allocate Income: Insufficient Income (LO 3)

Maryanne and Lisa pay each partner $25,000. Maryanne is to receive a $10,000 bonus because she originally contributed more capital and she works more hours. They each expect to receive 10% interest on their ending capital balance before allocating net income of $50,000 and $40,000 for Maryanne and Lisa, respectively. How is the net income allocated if the partnership earns $50,000?

Exercise 1-10

Admit New Partner: Comparison of Different Methods (LO 4)

Able and Baker are partners with capital balances of $200,000 and $80,000, respectively. Their income ratio is 8/2. They are planning on admitting Cathy to the partnership with a 20% interest. Prepare the journal entries that the partnership will record to admit Cathy as a partner. Evaluate each situation independently.
   a. Cathy gives Able $45,000 and Baker $25,000.
   b. Cathy contributes $120,000 to the partnership. The partnership uses the goodwill method.
   c. Cathy contributes $120,000 to the partnership. The partnership uses the bonus method.
   d. Cathy contributes $60,000 to the partnership. The partnership uses the bonus method.
   e. Cathy contributes $60,000 to the partnership. The partnership uses the goodwill method.

Exercise 1-11

Admit New Partner: Bonus Method (LO 4)

Peter and Mary want Paul to join their partnership. P&M's partnership agreement specifies the use of the **bonus method** for valuing the contribution of new partners. Peter and Mary have capital balances of $40,000 and $20,000, respectively. Paul will contribute $30,000 for a 30% interest.

    a. What journal entry will be recorded by the partnership for admitting Paul as a partner?

    b. After Paul joins the partnership, what profit-sharing ratio will each partner have?

Exercise 1-12

Admit New Partner: Goodwill Method (LO 4)

Peter and Mary want Paul to join their partnership. P&M's partnership agreement specifies the use of the **goodwill method** for valuing the contribution of new partners. Peter and Mary have capital balances of $40,000 and $20,000, respectively. Paul will contribute $30,000 for a 30% interest.

    a. What journal entry will be recorded by the partnership for admitting Paul as a partner?

    b. After Paul joins the partnership, what profit-sharing ratio will each partner have?

PROBLEMS

Problem 1-1

Form a Partnership (LO 2)

John, Adam, and Sally create a partnership. The partners contribute assets to the partnership with the following fair market values:

	Cash	Building	Land
John	$50,000		
Adam	$10,000	$40,000	
Sally			$50,000

Required:

    a. Prepare the journal entries to be recorded by the partnership to form the partnership.

    b. Prepare the partnership balance sheet upon formation.

Problem 1-2

Allocate Net Income (LO 3)

John, Adam, and Sally have written their partnership agreement. Based upon this agreement, John will receive an annual salary of $21,000 for managing the partnership. Adam and Sally will receive an 8% interest based upon their capital balances at the beginning of the year. Adam works extra hours and will receive a bonus of 10% of net income after the bonus. All partners had beginning capital balances of $50,000 and share income or losses equally.

Required:

    a. Prepare an income allocation schedule for the partners assuming annual Net Income is $88,000.

    b. Assume that during the year the partners withdraw amounts equal to their salary and amounts owed for interest on capital. What are the capital balances for the partners at the end of the year?

Problem 1-3   **Allocate Insufficient Net Income (LO 3)**

Jason, Andrew, and Sandra have a written partnership agreement. The agreement allows Jason to receive an annual salary of $30,000 for managing the partnership. All partners will receive 10% interest based upon their capital balances at the beginning of the year. Sandra works extra hours and will receive a bonus of 20% of net income after Jason's salary and the bonus. All partners had beginning capital balances of $120,000 and share income or losses equally.

Required:

a. Prepare an income allocation schedule for the partners assuming annual Net Income is $66,000.
b. Assume that during the year Jason withdrew an amount equal to his salary and interest on capital. What are the capital balances for the partners at the end of the year?

Problem 1-4   **Allocate Net Income: Partners Have Different Income-Sharing Ratio (LO 3)**

Alice, Ida, and Joshua are partners with a 3/3/4 profit-sharing ratio. The partnership agreement provides that each partner receives 6% interest on his or her weighted-average capital balance during the year. Alice and Ida receive salaries of $20,000 and $15,000, respectively. Joshua is entitled to a 10% bonus after salaries and bonus. The partners had beginning capital balances of $50,000, $40,000, and $30,000, respectively, for Alice, Ida, and Joshua. During the year, the partnership had net income of $156,000 and the following transactions occurred between the partners and the partnership:

April 1   Joshua contributed $20,000
July 1   Ida contributed $10,000
October 1   Each partner withdrew $15,000

Required:

a. Allocate the net income to the partners.
b. Compute the year-end capital balance for each partner.

Problem 1-5   **Admit New Partner: Comparison of Methods (LO 4)**

Johnson and Park have a partnership where they have capital balances of $120,000 and $60,000 and a 6/4 profit-sharing ratio, respectively. Randall is to join the partnership for a 25% interest.

Required:

a. After admitting Randall, what will be the resulting profit- and loss-sharing ratios for each partner?

For **independent scenarios b through h**, determine Randall's capital balance upon being admitted to the partnership. Also, where appropriate, indicate whether it is acceptable to use the bonus method or goodwill method.

b. Randall contributes $50,000, and total assets are not to be revalued.
c. Randall contributes $50,000, and total assets are not to be revalued; however, land is undervalued by $20,000.
d. Randall contributes $50,000, and total assets are not to be revalued; however, equipment is overvalued by $40,000.
e. Randall contributes $70,000, and total assets are not to be revalued.
f. Randall contributes $70,000, and total assets are to be revalued.
g. Randall contributes $70,000, and total assets are to be revalued when land is undervalued by $20,000.
h. Randall contributes $50,000, and total assets are being revalued.

Problem 1-6

Admit New Partner: Bonus Method (LO 4)

Johnson and Park have a partnership where they have capital balances of $120,000 and $60,000 and a 6/4 profit-sharing ratio, respectively. Randall is to contribute $80,000 to join the partnership. The land is undervalued $20,000, and the building is overvalued $40,000.

Required:

Prepare the partnership journal entries associated with admitting Randall to the partnership assuming the use of the bonus method.
   a. Randall receives a 20% interest.
   b. Randall receives a 40% interest.

Problem 1-7

Admit New Partner: Goodwill Method (LO 4)

Johnson and Park have a partnership where they have capital balances of $120,000 and $60,000 and a 6/4 profit-sharing ratio, respectively. Randall is to contribute $80,000 to join the partnership. The land is undervalued $20,000 and the building is overvalued $40,000.

Required:

Prepare the partnership journal entries associated with admitting Randall to the partnership assuming the use of the goodwill method.
   a. Randall receives a 20% interest.
   b. Randall receives a 40% interest.

Problem 1-8

Compare and Contrast Goodwill Method and Bonus Method (LO 4)

Samson and Goliath are partners with capital balances of $80,000 and $70,000, respectively. Delilah wants to join the partnership and offers them $30,000 for a 15% partnership interest. S&G have not specified in their partnership agreement the use of either the bonus or the goodwill method. Samson wants Delilah to have as large a capital balance as possible. They have come to you as an aspiring accountant to help them resolve this issue. What is your recommendation to S&G? Why?

Problem 1-9

Compare and Contrast Cash vs. Accrual Accounting Method (LO 1)

D&P Consulting is a professional service firm. The partners want to maximize their first year's net income. They don't know whether to use the cash or accrual basis. The partners know you are an accounting major and provide you with the following summarized information:

Billings to clients	$200,000
Collections from clients	$175,000
Supplies ordered	$ 30,000
Supplies used	$ 15,000
Amount paid to vendors for supplies	$ 20,000
Insurance paid (2 years)	$ 30,000
Rent paid (14 months)	$ 28,000
Salaries paid	$ 30,000
Salaries earned	$ 32,000

Required:

Write a memo to them explaining which accounting method you recommend. In the memo, include an explanation of how the different information supplied to you was used. You may use supporting schedules if you feel that is appropriate.

Problem 1-10

CASE: Problems 10 through 12 Relate to the Same Fact Pattern
Research Accounting Standards

Jen, Dorothy, and Nic have decided to open a children's book store. They were all education majors in college and love reading to children. They believe that they can have a retail store-front location as well as hold book fairs at various schools in the region. In forming a partnership, they each have some assets to contribute.

Jen has $30,000 in her savings account. Dorothy has a piece of property that she purchased for $30,000.

Nic has been following the price of GE stock since her grandparents gave her the shares. Her grandfather taught her to read the financial pages, and she knows the stock was worth $20,000 when she was given it. She knows the stock is currently worth $40,000.

The City has appraised Dorothy's land for $60,000. She is angry that she has to pay taxes based upon the $60,000 even though she has been provided with two independent appraisals for $50,000.

Since you're their friend from college, they are asking your advice on how to originally value the partnership. You promise to provide them with a beginning balance sheet, and you decide to begin the process by researching the accounting standards concerned with contributing assets to partnerships or exchanging non-monetary assets.

Required:

a. Prepare a memo summarizing your research concerning how the contributed assets should be valued.
b. Prepare a letter to the partners detailing how their contributions were valued. In this letter, include a balance sheet at formation of the partnership.

Problem 1-11

Operations: Create a System and Prepare Financial Statements

Use the beginning balances from the balance sheet completed in Problem 10. (If Problem 10 was not assigned, the professor will provide you with beginning capital balances.) During the year, the following transactions occurred for the Children's Book Store. Jen, Dorothy, and Nic have a profit-sharing ratio of 4/2/2.

Credit sales for the year	$150,000
Collections on account	$120,000
Inventory purchased from vendors on account	$ 90,000
Payments to vendors	$ 65,000
Payment for Rent	$ 24,000
Payment for Supplies	$ 8,000
Payments for Insurance	$ 6,000

Their gross margin on book sales is 60%.
Salaries paid to partners, $15,000 each

Required:

Prepare in proper form year-end financial statements.

Problem 1-12   **Provide Recommendation on Admitting New Partner**

Assume that Jen, Dorothy, and Nic have the capital balances of $30,000, $50,000, and $30,000, respectively. To obtain more cash, they plan on admitting Melanie as a 20% partner for $30,000.

Required:

Prepare a memo to the partners explaining the difference between the Goodwill Method and the Bonus Method. In the memo, provide capital balances upon admitting Melanie for both methods. Conclude the memo with a recommendation for one of the two methods. Prepare a balance sheet for the recommended method assuming the beginning balances are Cash $30,000 and Other Assets $80,000.

Problem 1-13   **Internet Assignment**

Accountants have a responsibility to limited partners. Provide a summary of the fiduciary relationship owed by accountants to the limited partners of a partnership when preparing financial statements. Use Lexus-Nexis to research this issue.

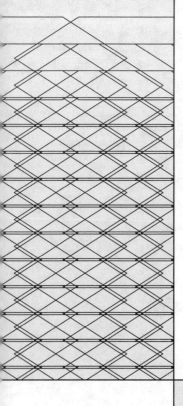

CHAPTER 2

LIQUIDATION OF A PARTNERSHIP

LEARNING OBJECTIVES

- Describe the process when a partner withdraws or retires from a partnership.
- Explain the difference between the withdrawal process and the liquidation process.
- Prepare a liquidation plan for either cash or on an installment basis.
- Explain the process for accounting for an insolvent partner.
- Compute a safe payment for each partner.

In Chapter 1, the general principle of "maintaining equity between partners" was established as the basis for partnership accounting. This principle was illustrated during partnership formation and the addition of partners. That discussion emphasized the need for partners to write a partnership agreement during formation. This document governs the partnership operation and the addition and the withdrawal of partners.

Establishing this document during formation is key because, at that time, the partners believe in the promise of the partnership and are very happy with each other. They are in a position to compromise with each other and to establish equitable guidelines. The time to discuss how to end a partnership is not when partners are disputing with each other or when the partnership needs to be dissolved or liquidated; it is when the organization is being formed.

Chapter 2 will discuss the issues associated with leaving a partnership. Partners may leave during operations to pursue other activities, to retire from the ongoing partnership, or at the end of the partnership when it is necessary to sell all the assets and liquidate the partnership. The general principle of "maintaining equity among the partners" will be continued. However, the need to protect partnership creditors is an important concern during the liquidation process.

This chapter will be organized to first discuss what happens when a partner withdraws from a partnership. Then the **Uniform Partnership Act (UPA)** basic principles of liquidating partnerships will be presented. The **lump-sum** and **installment liquidation processes** will then be examined. There will also be a discussion of a **safe-payments schedule** that allows for protection of partners and creditors during the installment process.

WITHDRAWAL OF A PARTNER (LO 1)

Existing partners may want to withdraw or retire from the partnership. The following section will discuss the issues associated with a partnership that will not continue and needs to be liquidated. This section will discuss the situation where the partnership theoretically is dissolved but, in fact, operations continue.

Let us assume that Anne, Bette, and Chris have a partnership with the following characteristics:

	Capital Balance	Profit Interest
Anne	$60,000	50%
Bette	$48,000	30%
Chris	$32,000	20%

Chris wants to withdraw from the partnership. The partnership has a number of options for handling the withdrawal similar to the options associated with admitting a new partner. Again, it is best to establish the procedures to be followed in the partnership agreement. The first option to be discussed involves the partners paying with personal funds outside of the partnership.

Using Funds External to the Partnership

Assuming the transaction is at book value then the following would be recorded on the partnership books:

Chris, Capital	32,000	
Anne, Capital		20,000
Bette, Capital		12,000

The journal entry does not involve cash because the payments were handled outside of the partnership. Also, notice that the capital allocation for Anne did not occur based on her original 50%. Instead, the allocation is based upon the relationship after Chris withdraws 50% and 30%, or 5/8 and 3/8, for Anne and Bette respectively.

Using Partnership Funds

Partnerships may also establish procedures to use partnership funds to buy out the withdrawing partner. The following examples examine situations where the payments are either greater than or less than the partnership's book value.

PAYMENTS IN EXCESS OF BOOK VALUE TO WITHDRAWING PARTNER The partnership agrees to pay Chris $48,000 for his interest. The amount paid the withdrawing partner could be in cash, with a note, or with another asset. A management issue arises if the partnership agrees to pay cash. The withdrawal of relatively large sums of cash may impact negatively the partnership's liquidity. Transactions of this type need to be planned.

Bonus Method

This transaction can be accounted for under either the bonus method or the goodwill method. Since the amount is in excess of the book value then the bonus is being paid to the withdrawing partner. Following the bonus method the transaction would be recorded by the partnership as:

Anne, Capital	10,000	
Bette, Capital	6,000	
Chris, Capital	32,000	
Cash (Notes Payable, etc.)		48,000

Goodwill Method

The goodwill method assumes that the partnership is being valued at its fair market value. The implied fair market value is computed by:

$$\text{Implied Market Value} = \frac{(\text{Payment to Withdrawing Partner} - \text{Partner's Capital Balance})}{\text{Partner's Profit Interest}}$$

$$\$80,000 = (\$48,000 - 32,000) = \$16,000/20\%$$

Recognizing goodwill in this instance creates some unresolved theoretical issues. One issue involves whether a continuing partnership's value can be increased because a partner is withdrawing. A second issue involves whether a withdrawal is really an arms-length transaction between independent parties that establishes an objective valuation. A partnership that decides to record goodwill will record it under one of two assumptions. One method would use the following entry:

Goodwill	16,000	
Chris, Capital	32,000	
Cash (Notes Payable, etc.)		48,000

This entry records goodwill only associated with the withdrawing partner. This theoretically is supported by the concept that only purchased goodwill is recorded. The second method would use the following entries:

Goodwill	80,000	
Anne, Capital		40,000
Bette, Capital		24,000
Chris, Capital		16,000
Chris, Capital	48,000	
Cash (Notes Payable, etc.)		48,000

This entry records the total goodwill based upon the implied market value for all of the partners. This is theoretically supported by the concept that the intangible asset should not be partially recorded but should be recorded in total.

PAYMENTS OF LESS THAN BOOK VALUE TO WITHDRAWING PARTNER The partnership agrees to pay Chris $30,000 for his interest. In this situation, Chris is receiving less than the book value. The bonus method implies that the remaining partners each receive a bonus to their capital accounts. The following partnership entry would be recorded in support of this method:

Chris, Capital	32,000	
Cash		30,000
Anne, Capital		1,250
Bette, Capital		750

Under the goodwill method, a payment of less than the partnership's book value implies that the assets are overvalued. Therefore, explicit impaired assets should be written down. In this situation, the implied partnership overvaluation is $10,000 ($2,000/20%).

Anne, Capital	5,000	
Bette, Capital	3,000	
Chris, Capital	2,000	
Assets		10,000
Chris, Capital	30,000	
Cash		30,000

The withdrawal or retirement of a partner should be planned as a normal course of a continuing business. The methods described have an underlying assumption that the partnership could be dissolved and then continue without the withdrawing partner. The next section discusses the situation when the partnership will no longer continue and is to be liquidated.

GUIDELINES FOR LIQUIDATING A PARTNERSHIP (LO 2)

While forming a partnership, the individual partners contribute assets to the partnership. These assets become the property of the partnership. The contribution increases the partner's capital account balance. During **liquidation**, the partnership needs to distribute the assets to the partners. However, before the partners can receive their liquidating payments, the partnership's liabilities must be eliminated. Also, during the liquidation process, potential liquidation expenses and gains or losses associated with the process must be allocated to the partners so that premature disbursements are not made. During the liquidation process, the principal decision-maker, either one of the partners or an outside trustee responsible for the process, can be held personally liable for improperly authorizing disbursements.

Ranking of Partnership Liabilities

The UPA provides that the assets of the partnership will be used to pay creditors and partners in the following rank order. Payments shall be made in the amount:

   I.   owing to creditors other than partners,
  II.   owing to partners other than from capital and profits,
 III. owing to partners in respect of capital,
 IV. owing to partners in respect of profits.

Applying these rules allows for a smooth liquidation process. A legal doctrine, *the right of offset*, provides that loans to partners be treated the same as partner capital and profits. Unless there are compelling economic reasons or specifications within the partnership agreement, the right of offset is applied. The following example demonstrates the importance of this doctrine. Partnership XYZ has assets of $20,000. Z is owed $30,000 by the partnership. The capital balances are:

  X $ 5,000
  Y $ 5,000
  Z   ($20,000)

If Z was treated as a creditor, then he would claim that the total assets of $20,000 were to be distributed to him in repayment of the loan. This would leave nothing for either X or Y.

If, however, the $30,000 loan offsets the debit capital balance first, then the resulting capital balances are:

  X $ 5,000
  Y $ 5,000
  Z $10,000

In this situation, the $20,000 can be distributed to the three partners. It can be seen that without the right of offset, Z with a debit capital balance would receive a distribution. This would then require the other partners, X and Y, to try and obtain funds from Z's personal assets.

Debit Capital Balances

The UPA calls for the partners to contribute personal assets necessary to satisfy unpaid partnership liabilities. If a partner cannot contribute personal assets then the other partners will contribute based upon their profit interest to cover the unpaid liabilities. This means that the partners are to make up any deficits in their capital accounts, and if they are insolvent and not capable of making up the difference the other partners will contribute on their behalf, based upon his or her respective profit interest.

As is true in other aspects of operating a partnership, the partnership agreement can establish explicit procedures to handle debit capital balances. Also, the UPA description applies to general partners. Limited partners, as discussed in Chapter 1, are at risk only for their invested capital. The rest of the discussion in this chapter assumes all partners are general partners, the partnership agreement follows the UPA, and the partners will repay debit balances.

Marshaling of Assets

The requirement to contribute personal assets to pay partnership liabilities illustrates the concept of **unlimited liability** covered in Chapter 1. However, another legal doctrine, the *Marshaling of Assets*, is applied when the partnership or one or more of the partners is insolvent. This doctrine protects secured creditors or others who have filed liens by:

- allowing partnership assets to first cover partnership creditors. Any excess of partnership assets over partnership liabilities can be used to cover personal liabilities but only to the extent of the partner's capital balance. Personal assets are used to pay personal creditors prior to obligations associated with the partnership.
- establishing a rank order for distributing the property of partners who have declared bankruptcy. Amounts owed will be paid in the following order:
  i.   personal creditors,
  ii. partnership creditors,
  iii. partners by way of contribution.

The amount owed to partners by way of contribution refers to the need of the partners to contribute to the partnership for any debit capital balances. For example, assume there are two partners, Abbey and Bette, that are in the following situation:

	(All Cash) Personal Assets	Personal Liabilities	Capital Balances
Abbey	$30,000	$10,000	($15,000)
Bette	$50,000	$40,000	($20,000)

In this situation, Abbey has sufficient personal assets to cover her personal liabilities and to cover a $15,000 deficit in her partnership capital account. Bette has enough personal assets to cover her personal liabilities but can only contribute $10,000 towards the deficit in her partnership account.

■ CONCEPTUAL QUESTION AND REFLECTION

Partners will have business and personal interests outside of the partnership. In Chapter 1, the point was made that partners have personal assets at risk associated with the partnership. Partner A, of the A&B partnership, is having financial difficulties. A is delinquent on a $10,000 note to the First Federal Bank. In the process of liquidating their partnership, A&B sold a building for $40,000. They owe First Federal $30,000 on a mortgage associated with the building. The bank wants A&B to turn over the extra $10,000 of proceeds from selling the building in satisfaction of A's Note. Do you believe that the bank has the right to claim payment by the partnership of A's Note as well as the repayment of the mortgage?

LUMP SUM LIQUIDATION (LO 3)

The intent of dissolving the partnership is to liquidate the assets, pay off the creditors, and return the capital balances to the partners. The lump-sum process provides for all partners to receive only one payment at the end. Therefore, it is not possible to have a premature distribution to an individual partner.

After five years of operations, April, Leo, and Shari have decided to end their partnership. Their profit and loss ratios are 40%/40%/20%, and their balance sheet contains the following items:

Cash	$ 50,000	Accounts Payable, Trade	$ 15,000
Accounts Receivable, Clients	$ 80,000	Notes Payable, April	$ 40,000
Accounts Receivable, Leo	$ 30,000	April, Capital	$ 60,000
Equipment, Net	$ 35,000	Leo, Capital	$ 50,000
		Sheri, Capital	$ 30,000
		Total Liabilities and	
Total Assets	$195,000	Partners' Capital	$195,000

Example: Assuming No Gains or Losses

Assume that the receivables are collected in full; the equipment will be distributed to April and the book value equals fair market value. Table 2-1 displays the transactions that are explained below. The format of this schedule follows the basic accounting equation Assets = Liabilities + Owners' Capital. Notice that the Total Capital column equals the sum of the partners' capital accounts. All transactions that impact the capital accounts are shown against the total capital and then the separate capital accounts. The concept is that the accounts should always balance.

(a) Applying the *right of offset* to April's Note to the partnership: The $40,000 is added to her partnership capital.
(b) After each transaction, the accounts can be subtotaled to show the schedule is in balance.
(c) Applying the *right of offset* to Leo's loan from the partnership: The $30,000 is deducted from his partnership capital.
(d) The asset accounts receivable was collected at book value, so there was no gain or loss. This assumes that the partnership records are kept using the accrual method. If the partnership used the cash basis, then the collection of accounts receivable would represent income to the individual partners and would need to be allocated to each partner's capital account.

(e) If there are no transactions against the capital columns, then it is not necessary to keep subtotaling the separate partner's accounts.

(f) Cash was used to satisfy the liabilities.

(g) The equipment was distributed to April. Since book value equaled fair market value, there was no gain or loss to the partnership nor an impact against the other partners. It is acceptable to distribute assets other than cash to partners. The impact of the distribution of assets other than cash depends upon a variety of tax attributes associated with the property. This topic is discussed in more detail in Chapter 3.

(h) At this point, the schedule contains only the asset cash $115,000 equal to Total Capital of $115,000. Also, each of the partnership capital accounts is positive (credit balance). A necessary condition to distribute cash to the partners is for the schedule to show only the asset cash and that no partner has a debit balance.

(i) Cash is distributed to the partners resulting in zero ($0) balances for all of the partnership accounts. The partnership has been liquidated.

TABLE 2-1: Lump-Sum Liquidation with No Gains or Losses

Description of the Transaction	Cash	Other Assets	Liabilities	Total Capital	April, Capital 40%	Leo, Capital 40%	Sheri, Capital 20%
Beginning Balance	50,000	145,000	55,000	140,000	60,000	50,000	30,000
(a) Partner's Loan			(40,000)	40,000	40,000		
(b) Subtotal	50,000	145,000	15,000	180,000	100,000	50,000	30,000
(c) Partner's A/R		(30,000)		(30,000)		(30,000)	
Subtotal	50,000	115,000	15,000	150,000	100,000	20,000	30,000
(d) Collect A/R	80,000	(80,000)					
(e) Subtotal	130,000	35,000	15,000	150,000			
(f) Pay Liabilities	(15,000)		(15,000)				
Subtotal	115,000	35,000	0	150,000			
(g) Distribute Equipment		(35,000)		(35,000)	(35,000)		
(h) Subtotal	115,000	0	0	115,000	65,000	20,000	30,000
(i) Distribute Cash	(115,000)			(115,000)	(65,000)	(20,000)	(30,000)
Ending Balances	0	0	0	0	0	0	0

WITHDRAWAL AND EXPULSION OF PARTNERS FROM LAW FIRMS

Some of the social forces impacting change in law firms include[1]:

- Changes in the character of the practice of law including specialization; obsolescence in legal knowledge acquired in law school compared to the current knowledge needed to practice in later stages of a professional career; and increased competition.
- Changing organizational structures needed to perform specific professional services, including the establishment of non-legal office situations such as in-house corporation lawyers, governmental departments, and large prosecutorial offices.
- Establishment of increasingly larger firms, many organized as limited liability entities, with separate operational and administrative functions.

(continued on next page)

> The economics of allocating revenue is typically the underlying reason for dissolution of law firms. Intergenerational conflict concerning junior partners believing they are carrying the workload rather than the more senior partners is a classic example. Another economic problem area relates to the allocation of revenues between specialties that do not generate as high a level of revenue.
>
> The issues discussed above concerning law firms can also be discussed related to CPA firms. The need to constantly reallocate revenues is necessary to reduce tensions among partners. This is especially true as junior partners increasingly develop not only their technical skills but also their interpersonal abilities. The junior partners believe that their contributions have increased and expect to be compensated accordingly.
>
> Developing allocation schemes is an important aspect of keeping large professional service partnerships together. Small firms can dissolve and begin again; large firms need to provide for mechanisms to allow for partners to equitably withdraw or, if necessary, to be expelled from the firms.
>
> [1]"The Underlying Causes of Withdrawal and Expulsion of Partners from Law Firms," Geoffrey C. Hazard, Jr., *Washington & Lee Law Review*, Fall 1998, pp. 1073 – 1081.

ACCOUNTING FOR AN INSOLVENT PARTNER (LO 4)

The prior example assumes that all assets were disposed of at book value (no gains or losses). This is typically an unrealistic assumption. Businesses will usually need to be liquidated in a short period of time. However, needing to sell assets quickly typically will not result in the assets being disposed at their best value.

Example: Assuming Gains and Losses while Accounting for an Insolvent Partner

Assume that the partnership is being liquidated due to Leo not following all of his duties as a partner. For instance, he has not been collecting what is due from his clients. Therefore, only $20,000 of the receivables can be collected. Assume the equipment is sold at an auction for $41,000. In addition, there are legal fees of $5,000 associated with the liquidation. Leo has no personal assets outside of his investment in the partnership. Table 2-2 displays the transactions as discussed below.

(a) Applying the *right of offset* to April's Note to the partnership: The $40,000 is added to her partnership capital.

(b) Applying the *right of offset* to Leo's loan from the partnership: The $30,000 is deducted from his partnership capital.

(c) Only $20,000 of the asset accounts receivable was collected. The remaining $60,000 was not collected and was treated as a loss on disposal of an asset. This was allocated to the partners' capital accounts based upon their profit interest.

(d) Cash was used to satisfy the liabilities.

(e) The equipment was sold for $41,000. Since book value was $35,000, this is a $6,000 gain that is allocated to the partners' capital accounts based upon their profit interest.

(f) The $5,000 in legal fees was paid and the expense was allocated to the partners' capital accounts based upon their profit interest.

(g) At this point, the schedule contains only the asset cash $91,000 equal to Total Capital of $91,000. However, the process did not reach the necessary condition of having only cash and no partner debit balances. Leo has a $3,600 debit balance (negative balance). Based upon the UPA, he is supposed to contribute the difference. In this case, he does not have any outside assets and is not capable of meeting his obligation to the partnership. Therefore, remaining partners April and Sheri need to cover the difference. Leo's debit balance is allocated to these two partners based upon their remaining profit and loss ratios, 40%/20%. Based upon the doctrine of *marshaling of assets*, there are no partnership assets available for Leo's personal creditors.

(h) The debit balance was allocated to April and Sheri based upon a 2/3 (40/60), 1/3 (20/60) ratio, respectively. Note the allocation to April = 2/3 * 3,600 = 2,400.

(i) Cash is distributed to the partners resulting in zero ($0) balances for all of the partnership accounts. The partnership has been liquidated.

TABLE 2·2: Lump-Sum Liquidation with Gains and Losses

Description of the Transaction	Cash	Other Assets	Liabilities	Total Capital	April, Capital 40%	Leo, Capital 40%	Sheri, Capital 20%
Beginning Balance	50,000	145,000	55,000	140,000	60,000	50,000	30,000
(a) Partner's Loan			(40,000)	40,000	40,000		
Subtotal	50,000	145,000	15,000	180,000	100,000	50,000	30,000
(b) Partner's A/R		(30,000)		(30,000)		(30,000)	
Subtotal	50,000	115,000	15,000	150,000	100,000	20,000	30,000
(c) Collect A/R	20,000	(80,000)		(60,000)	(24,000)	(24,000)	(12,000)
Subtotal	70,000	35,000	15,000	90,000	76,000	(4,000)	18,000
(d) Pay Liabilities	(15,000)		(15,000)				
Subtotal	55,000	35,000	0	90,000			
(e) Auction Equipment	41,000	(35,000)		6,000	2,400	2,400	1,200
Subtotal	96,000	0	0	96,000	78,400	(1,600)	19,200
(f) Liquidation Expenses	(5,000)			(5,000)	(2,000)	(2,000)	(1,000)
(g) Subtotal	91,000	0	0	91,000	76,400	(3,600)	18,200
(h) Allocate Debit Balance					(2,400)	3,600	(1,200)
Subtotal	91,000			91,000	74,000	0	17,000
(i) Distribute Cash	(91,000)			(91,000)	(74,000)	0	(17,000)
Ending Balances	0	0	0	0	0	0	0

With a **lump-sum liquidation schedule**, all of the transactions listed above would be recorded in the partnership accounting records. The following journal entries would be recorded for transactions (h) and (i):

(h) April, Capital   2,400
    Sheri, Capital   1,200
        Leo, Capital   3,600

Eliminate Leo's debit balance by allocating this amount to April and Sheri.

(i) April, Capital   74,000
    Sheri, Capital   17,000
        Cash   91,000

Distribute remaining cash to April and Sheri based upon their capital account balances.

■ CONCEPTUAL QUESTION AND REFLECTION

> Assume Leo did have personal assets of $5,000 outside the partnership. He owes personal creditors $2,000. Should Leo contribute $3,000 to the partnership?

INSTALLMENT LIQUIDATION (LO 3)

The lump-sum liquidation process assumes that the partners will receive their distribution after all other partnership affairs have been finalized. The liquidation process can sometimes take many months or years to dispose of all of the assets. Partners may want to receive funds as they become available. Of course, as discussed earlier, there is always the concern of a premature distribution. To prevent the possibility of premature distributions, the Plan of Distributions will usually include the preparation of a **safe-payments schedule**. The first example provides an example of the installment process and does not include the preparation of the safe-payments schedule.

Illustration of Installment Method without a Safe-Payments Schedule

Let us return to the first example of dissolving the *A&L* partnership. In this case, there were no losses associated with the collection of the receivables. Table 2-3 displays the information associated with the following transactions that assume the liquidation starts in January, the equipment can be disposed of in June, and receivables are collected as follows:

January 31	$25,000
February 25	$10,000
March 15	$30,000
June 15	$15,000

The legal expenses are due in June. The partners expect to receive distributions on March 1 and July 1. The March 1 distribution is only for $30,000.

(a) Applying the *right of offset* to April's Note to the partnership: The $40,000 is added to her partnership capital.
(b) Applying the *right of offset* to Leo's loan from the partnership: The $30,000 is deducted from his partnership capital.
(c) $25,000 of the asset accounts receivable was collected.
(d) The liabilities were satisfied.
(e) $10,000 of the asset accounts receivable was collected.
(f) Distribute $30,000 to partners. This example should point out the problems with a premature distribution: April has a $100,000 capital balance and Leo has a $20,000 capital balance. If we assume that partners get a distribution based upon their profit interest, then April and Leo will each receive $12,000. This will leave Leo with only a capital balance of $8,000. However, if the remaining assets, $80,000 (receivables of $45,000 and equipment for $35,000) cannot be sold for at least book value, then Leo should be expected to cover an anticipated loss of $32,000. This is not an equitable way for the partners to treat each other. Hopefully, the conceptual issues are obvious and it can be seen that this particular example should not occur in practice.

(g) March 15: $30,000 collection of accounts receivable.
(h) $15,000 of the asset accounts receivable was collected.
(i) Legal Expenses of $5,000 were paid.
(j) Equipment was sold for $35,000.
(k) Cash was distributed to partners.

TABLE 2-3: Installment Liquidation with No Gains or Losses

Description of the Transaction	Cash	Other Assets	Liabilities	Total Capital	April, Capital 40%	Leo, Capital 40%	Sheri, Capital 20%
Beginning Balance	50,000	145,000	55,000	140,000	60,000	50,000	30,000
(a) Partner's Loan			(40,000)	40,000	40,000		
Subtotal	50,000	145,000	15,000	180,000	100,000	50,000	30,000
(b) Partner's A/R		(30,000)		(30,000)		(30,000)	
Subtotal	50,000	115,000	15,000	150,000	100,000	20,000	30,000
(c) Collect A/R	25,000	(25,000)					
Subtotal	75,000	90,000	15,000	150,000			
(d) Pay Liabilities	(15,000)		(15,000)				
Subtotal	60,000	90,000	0	150,000			
(e) Collect A/R	10,000	(10,000)					
Subtotal	70,000	80,000	0	150,000	100,000	20,000	30,000
(f) Distribute Cash March 15	(30,000)			(30,000)	(12,000)	(12,000)	(6,000)
Subtotal	40,000	80,000	0	120,000	88,000	8,000	24,000
(g) Collect A/R	30,000	(30,000)					
Subtotal	70,000	50,000	0	120,000			
(h) Collect A/R	15,000	(15,000)					
Subtotal	85,000	35,000	0	120,000			
(i) Pay Legal Fees	(5,000)			(5,000)	(2,000)	(2,000)	(1,000)
Subtotal	80,000	35,000	0	115,000	86,000	6,000	23,000
(j) Sell Equipment	35,000	(35,000)					
Subtotal	115,000	0	0	115,000			
(k) Distribute Cash	(114,000)			(115,000)	(86,000)	(6,000)	(23,000)
Ending Balances	0	0	0	0	0	0	0

SAFE-PAYMENTS SCHEDULE (LO 5)

As discussed in item (f) above, the disbursement of $30,000 was not an equitable treatment of the partners. Instead of computing the $30,000 payment based upon the profit interest, a safe-payments schedule could have been computed as of March 15. This schedule is prepared assuming that the remaining assets would not generate any further cash. The schedule, Figure 2-1, shows that as of March 15, all of the cash could be distributed between April $56,667 and Sheri $8,333 without making any premature payments.

FIGURE 2·1: A&L Partnership, Safe-Payments Schedule, March 15, 20xx

	April, Capital 40%	Leo, Capital 40%	Sheri, Capital 20%	Total Capital
Capital Balances (after recording items a through e)	100,000	20,000	30,000	150,000
Assumed Legal Fees for the Liquidation	(2,000)	(2,000)	(1,000)	(5,000)
Subtotal	98,000	18,000	29,000	145,000
Assumed Loss on Disposal of Assets	(32,000)	(32,000)	(16,000)	(80,000)
Subtotal	66,000	(14,000)	13,000	65,000
Allocation of Debit Balances	(9,333)	14,000	(4,667)	0
Safe-payments amounts	56,667	0	8,333	65,000

During an installment liquidation, the safe-payments schedule is prepared in support of the distribution plan. The assumed transactions would not be recorded in the partnership records. Example journal entries are included in the following comprehensive example.

■ **CONCEPTUAL QUESTION AND REFLECTION**

On March 15, the partnership cannot estimate the legal fees associated with the liquidation. Should they distribute any cash?

Comprehensive Illustration of Safe-Payments Schedule and Installment Liquidation

Molly, Mary, and Mel are equal partners in M³. They are going to dissolve their partnership. Information about the partnership and the individual partners includes:

M³ Balance Sheet

Cash	$ 10,000	Accounts Payable	$ 30,000
Accounts Receivable	$ 80,000	Mortgage Payable	$ 80,000
Investments	$ 30,000	Molly, Capital	$ 60,000
Building	$100,000	Mary, Capital	$ 30,000
		Mel, Capital	$ 20,000
		Total Liabilities &	
Total Assets	$220,000	Capital	$220,000

Personal Information outside of M³:

	Assets	Liabilities
Molly	30,000	10,000
Mary	21,000	20,000
Mel	10,000	40,000

The liquidation process is expected to start January 1, and Mel wants as much cash as possible. At the end of the liquidation process, there will be unpaid legal fees of $9,000. During January, $30,000 of receivables was collected. Can Mel be paid her capital balance at the end of January?

FIGURE 2-2: M³ Safe-Payments Schedule, January 31, 20xx

	Molly, Capital ⅓	Mary, Capital ⅓	Mel, Capital ⅓	Total Capital
Capital Balances	60,000	30,000	20,000	110,000
Assumed Legal Fees for the Liquidation	(3,000)	(3,000)	(3,000)	(9,000)
Subtotal	57,000	27,000	17,000	101,000
Assumed Loss on Disposal of Assets	(70,000)	(70,000)	(70,000)	(210,000)
Subtotal	(13,000)	(43,000)	(53,000)	(109,000)
Safe-payments amounts	0	0	0	0

The M³ Safe-Payments Schedule as of January 31, 20xx (Figure 2-2) shows that there is insufficient cash to allow any of the partners to receive any cash payments as of January 31. Note that if the partnership were liquidated, as of January 31 Molly is the only partner that is not insolvent and she would have to contribute personal assets to repay any unpaid liabilities.

The installment liquidation schedule for the following transactions is shown in Table 2-4.

(a) January Collection of A/R $30,000
(b) February Collection of receivables $35,000
(c) Sold building during February for $91,000
(d) Paid off mortgage
(e) March 1 Distribution of cash to partners
To distribute cash to the partners, a safe-payments schedule needs to be completed (see Figure 2-3). The first step is to determine the amount of cash that is available for distribution. In this situation, $47,000 of cash is available per the following schedule:

Cash Balance, Feb. 28:	$86,000
Outstanding Liabilities	(30,000)
Expected Legal Fees	(9,000)
Cash Available	$47,000

Even though all of the liabilities have not been paid as of February 28, cash up to $47,000 can be distributed. If the partners want to provide for unforeseen expenses, they can figure a contingency into their safe-payments schedule.

The March 1 cash distribution to the partners would be recorded in the partnership records with the following journal entry and explanation:

Molly, Capital	38,500	
Mary, Capital	8,500	
Cash		47,000

To distribute available cash to Molly and Mary based upon the M³ Safe-Payments Schedule dated February 28, 20xx (Figure 2-3).

FIGURE 2·3: M³ Safe-Payments Schedule, February 28, 20xx

	Molly, Capital ⅓	Mary, Capital ⅓	Mel, Capital ⅓	Total Capital
Capital Balances, Feb. 28	57,000	27,000	17,000	101,000
Assumed Legal Fees for the Liquidation	(3,000)	(3,000)	(3,000)	(9,000)
Subtotal	54,000	24,000	14,000	92,000
Assumed Loss on Disposal of Assets	(15,000)	(15,000)	(15,000)	(45,000)
Subtotal	39,000	9,000	(1,000)	47,000
Allocation of Debit Balances	(500)	(500)	1,000	0
Safe-payments amounts	38,500	8,500	0	47,000

   (f) Paid the liabilities
   (g) Sold Investments during March for $42,000
   (h) Determined that the remaining accounts receivable were worthless
   (i) Paid the legal fees
   (j) Final cash distribution to the partners. Note that while Mel received cash during the final distribution, she was not entitled to distribution prior to the end.

The following would be the final journal entry posted to the partnership ledger.

Molly, Capital	14,500	
Mary, Capital	14,500	
Mel, Capital	13,000	
Cash		42,000

■ CONCEPTUAL QUESTION AND REFLECTION

As stated in Chapter 1, a partnership does not have to use GAAP when preparing financial statements. A partnership can use the cash basis or accrual method as discussed in Chapter 1. Also, a partnership could report in their financial statements based upon how they file the tax return. This later method is referred to as the *tax-return basis* of accounting. Is the M³ Partnership using the cash basis, tax-return basis, or accrual method of accounting?

TABLE 2·4: Installment Liquidation for M³

Description of the Transaction	Cash	Other Assets	Liabilities	Total Capital	Molly, Capital ⅓	Mary, Capital ⅓	Mel, Capital ⅓
Beginning Balance	10,000	210,000	110,000	110,000	60,000	30,000	20,000
(a) Collect A/R – Jan.	30,000	(30,000)					
Subtotal Jan. 31	40,000	180,000	110,000	110,000			
(b) Collect A/R – Feb.	35,000	(35,000)					
(c) Sold Building	91,000	(100,000)		(9,000)	(3,000)	(3,000)	(3,000)
(d) Pay Mortgage	(80,000)		(80,000)				
Subtotal Feb. 28	86,000	45,000	30,000	101,000	57,000	27,000	17,000

(e) March 1 Cash Distribution to Partners	(47,000)			(47,000)	(38,500)	(8,500)	
Subtotal	39,000	45,000	30,000	54,000	18,500	18,500	17,000
(f) Pay Liabilities	(30,000)		(30,000)				
(g) Sold Investments	42,000	(30,000)		12,000	4,000	4,000	4,000
Subtotal	51,000	15,000	0	66,000	22,500	22,500	21,000
(h) Write-off A/R		(15,000)		(15,000)	(5,000)	(5,000)	(5,000)
Subtotal	51,000	0	0	51,000	17,500	17,500	16,000
(i) Pay Legal Fees	(9,000)			(9,000)	(3,000)	(3,000)	(3,000)
Subtotal	42,000	0	0	42,000	14,500	14,500	13,000
(j) Distribute Cash	(42,000)			(42,000)	(14,500)	(14,500)	(13,000)
Ending Balances	0	0	0	0	0	0	0

● **INTERPRETIVE EXERCISE**

Assume the same situation as above with the investments being worthless and the legal fees as $12,000. How much cash would Mel receive? How is it possible that the partnership is classifying Investments with a $30,000 balance that become worthless during the liquidation process?

SUMMARY

The **Learning Objectives** for this chapter were:

- Describe the process when a partner withdraws or retires from a partnership.
- Explain the difference between the withdrawal process and the liquidation process.
- Prepare a liquidation plan for either cash or on an installment basis.
- Explain the process for accounting for an insolvent partner.
- Compute a safe payment for each partner.

Describe the process when a partner withdraws or retires from a partnership.
When a partner withdraws or retires from the partnership, the partnership is assumed to be dissolved, but it is not liquidated. The remaining partners can pay for the withdrawal of a partner from either their personal funds or from partnership funds. This section examined the situation where Chris wanted to leave the ABC partnership and, thus, leaving Anne and Bette. Accounting procedures used under both the bonus and goodwill methods were discussed. It was mentioned that recording goodwill when a partner retires theoretically leaves some unexplained issues.

Explain the difference between the withdrawal process and the liquidation process.
This section discussed protecting the rights of partnership creditors and partners during the process of dissolving or liquidating a partnership. The *right of offset* for partner receivables and loans was explained through an example discussing the XYZ Partnership. The need for partners to cover any debit capital balances illustrates **unlimited liability**. The *marshaling of assets* doctrine is applied when one or more of the partners are insolvent.

Prepare a liquidation plan for either cash or on an installment basis.

Two methods of liquidating partnerships were discussed: *lump-sum* and *installment*. The lump-sum method assumes only one final payment to the partners after reconciling all of the partnership affairs. The lump-sum liquidation was discussed with an example of liquidating the *A&L* partnership assuming no gains or losses (Table 2-1).

The installment method allows for the partners to receive partial distributions during the liquidation process. To properly distribute funds, a **safe-payments schedule** should be prepared. The installment liquidation method was discussed as it related to an example of liquidating the *A&L* partnership without a safe-payments schedule (Table 2-3) as well as examples with the use of a safe-payments schedule (Figure 2-1).

Explain the process for accounting for an insolvent partner.

A partner is obligated to repay any debit balances to the partnership. However, if a partner is insolvent and has more personal debts than personal assets, then this repayment cannot always occur. The other partners are then responsible for covering the debit balance. This was discussed with an example associated with liquidating the *A&L* partnership assuming gains or losses on disposing of the partnership assets (Table 2-2).

Compute a safe payment for each partner.

The safe-payments schedule protects the partner or trustee responsible for liquidating the partnership by assuring that a premature distribution to the partners does not occur. The importance of a safe-payments schedule was discussed as it related to liquidating the *A&L* partnership without a safe-payments schedule. The proper use of the safe-payments schedule (Figures 2-2 and 2-3) was discussed with the comprehensive example associated with liquidating M^3 (Table 2-4).

QUESTIONS

1. John of the JK&L partnership wants to sell his interest in JK&L. What options are available to him for selling his partnership interest?
2. DEF is an existing partnership. D is going to withdraw. What concerns would E and F have related to D's leaving the partnership?
3. What does it mean to liquidate a partnership?
4. The UPA explicitly provides for a ranking of partnership liabilities. Describe this ranking.
5. Explain the impact that the *right of offset* has related to liquidating partnerships.
6. What rights do partners with a debit balance have?
7. *Marshaling of assets* is a legal doctrine applied when the partnership is faced with what financial condition?
8. During the liquidation of a cash basis partnership, an accounts receivable for $10,000 was collected. If the three partners A, B, and C have a profit ratio of 4/3/3, then how much of the $10,000 does A receive?
9. A partnership is liquidating, and a CPA is preparing a schedule in support of a partner distribution. Explain how the CPA knows when the schedule has been completed.
10. Partner A has a 30% profit interest in a partnership that is liquidating. Ignoring tax effects, what is the impact on A if equipment with a $30,000 carrying value is sold for book value?
11. Partner A has a 30% profit interest in a partnership that is liquidating. Ignoring tax effects, what is the impact on A if equipment with a $30,000 carrying value is sold for a fair market value of $40,000?
12. Partner A has a 30% profit interest in a partnership that is liquidating. Ignoring tax effects, what is the impact on A if equipment with a $30,000 carrying value is sold for a fair market value of $20,000?

13. Describe the impact on a liquidating partnership if a partner with a debit balance has no personal assets to contribute to the process.
14. When is it appropriate to prepare a safe-payments schedule?
15. A partner has a $30,000 capital balance. She wants to receive a distribution when partnership assets equal $100,000. The partnership agreement requires an installment liquidation process. As the partnership's accountant, what is your recommendation?

EXERCISES

Exercise 2-1

Multiple Choice—Select the best answer for each of the following.

1. The UPA ranks a payment owed to a creditor as a higher priority than a payment owed to a partner. For transactions with partners, payments are ranked higher related to amounts owed
   a. from partners other than capital and profits.
   b. to partners other than capital and profits.
   c. to partnership for capital.
   d. to partnership for profits.

2. Marshaling of assets is important when a partnership is insolvent. Which of the following groups is protected?
   a. personal creditors
   b. partnership creditors
   c. partners
   d. secured creditors

3. J, K, and L share profits as equal partners. J, K, and L's capital balances are currently $70,000, $60,000, and $50,000, respectively. In withdrawing from the partnership, L is paid $60,000 by J and K. Which is the journal entry recorded by the partnership?
   a. L, Capital   50,000
          J, Capital   25,000
          K, Capital   25,000
   b. L, Capital   60,000
          J, Capital   25,000
          K, Capital   25,000
          Cash   10,000
   c. L, Capital   60,000
          Cash   60,000
   d. L, Capital   50,000
          Cash   50,000

4. During liquidation of a cash basis partnership, the partnership collects an accounts receivable for $10,000. If the partners A, B, and C have a profit-sharing ratio of 4/3/3, how much is allocated to A?
   a. 10,000
   b. 6,000
   c. 4,000
   d. 0

5. During liquidation of an accrual basis partnership, the partnership collects an accounts receivable for $10,000. If the partners A, B, and C have a profit-sharing ratio of 4/3/3, how much is allocated to A?
   a. 10,000
   b. 6,000
   c. 4,000
   d. 0

Use the following information to answer questions 6 through 11.

A, B, and C share profits 30%/30%/40%, and they decide to liquidate their partnership while it has the following balances:

Cash	Accounts Receivable	Equipment	Accounts Receivable from A	Accounts Payable	Notes Payable to B	Total Capital	A Capital 30%	B Capital 30%	C Capital 40%
50,000	70,000	20,000	20,000	40,000	10,000	110,000	40,000	20,000	50,000

6. After applying the right of offset, A's Capital balance will be:
   a. 60,000
   b. 20,000
   c. 46,000
   d. 34,000
7. After applying the right of offset, B's Capital balance will be:
   a. 23,000
   b. 17,000
   c. 10,000
   d. 30,000
8. After collecting $30,000 of the accounts receivable, how much profit is allocated to C?
   a. 30,000
   b. 18,000
   c. 12,000
   d. 0
9. They sold the equipment for $5,000. How much profit or loss is allocated to C?
   a. Loss 6,000
   b. Loss 2,000
   c. Profit 6,000
   d. Profit 2,000
10. They pay off their liabilities. How much profit or loss is allocated to B?
    a. 0
    b. Loss 12,000
    c. Profit 12,000
    d. Loss 40,000
11. After collecting the remainder of the receivables and assuming that the activities in Questions 9 and 10 occurred, how much cash will A receive?
    a. 35,500
    b. 15,500
    c. 20,000
    d. 24,500

Exercise 2-2

Partner Withdrawal: Bonus Method (LO 1)

Alexander, Brian, and Christopher are partners with the following capital balances and profit interests:

	Capital Balance	Profit Interest
Alexander	$80,000	40%
Brian	$60,000	30%
Christopher	$40,000	30%

The partnership uses the **bonus method** when partners are admitted or withdraw. Christopher would like to withdraw from the partnership. Prepare journal entries for each of the following independent situations.
   a. The partnership agrees to pay Christopher $61,000 for his interest.
   b. The partnership agrees to pay Christopher $33,000 for his interest.

Exercise 2-3

Liquidation Journal Entries (LO 2)

Peter and Mary are partners who share profits equally. They decide to liquidate their partnership with the following balance sheet:

Cash	$30,000	Accounts Payable	$20,000
Land	$40,000	Peter, Capital	$30,000
		Mary, Capital	$20,000
		Total Liabilities and	
Total Assets	$70,000	Partners' Capital	$70,000

The partnership sells the land for $50,000, pays the liabilities, and distributes the remaining cash to the partners.

Required:

Prepare the journal entries recorded by the partnership.

Exercise 2-4

Lump-Sum Liquidation (LO 3)

Johnson and Lever are partners who split profits 60/40, respectively. They decide to liquidate the partnership when they have the following balances:

Cash	$20,000
Equipment	$30,000
Accounts Payable	$25,000
Johnson, Capital	$20,000
Lever, Capital	$ 5,000

During the liquidation, they sell the equipment for $10,000, pay off all of the partnership debts, and then distribute the remaining cash to the partners.

Required:

a. Prepare a lump-sum distribution schedule, assuming that Lever has sufficient personal assets to cover any debts owed the partnership.
b. Prepare a lump-sum distribution schedule, assuming that Lever is personally insolvent and cannot cover any debts owed the partnership.

Exercise 2-5

Liquidation Plan (LO 3)

Peter and Mary have decided to liquidate their partnership with the following balance sheet:

Cash	$30,000	Accounts Payable	$20,000
Land	$40,000	Peter, Capital	$30,000
		Mary, Capital	$20,000
		Total Liabilities and	
Total Assets	$70,000	Partners' Capital	$70,000

The liquidation process will take at least six months to profitably sell the land.

Required:

a. How much cash can each partner immediately receive?
b. If at the end of six months the land is sold for $50,000, how much cash will each partner receive at that time?

Exercise 2-6

Liquidation Plan with Safe-Payments Schedule (LO 3 & LO 5)

Peter and Mary have decided to liquidate their partnership with the following balance sheet:

Cash	$30,000	Accounts Payable	$20,000
Land	$40,000	Peter, Capital	$30,000
		Mary, Capital	$20,000
		Total Liabilities and	
Total Assets	$70,000	Partners' Capital	$70,000

The liquidation process will take at least six months to profitably sell the land. They recognize that they will need to keep at least $5,000 on hand to cover expenses that may occur.

Required:

    a. How much cash can each partner immediately receive? (Hint: prepare a safe-payments schedule)

    b. If at the end of six months the land is sold for $50,000, how much cash will each partner receive at that time?

Exercise 2-7

Liquidation Plan with Non-Equal Profit-Sharing Ratio (LO 3)

Jones and Smith are partners with a 3/2 profit-sharing ratio. They have capital balances of $50,000 and $40,000, respectively. They have cash of $20,000. The assets other than cash are sold for $100,000. How much does each partner receive during the liquidation?

Exercise 2-8

Lump-Sum Liquidation (LO 3)

Tony and Ken have a partnership with the following balance sheet:

Cash	$ 20,000	Accounts Payable	$ 30,000
Accounts Receivable	$ 50,000	Tony, Capital	$ 40,000
Equipment	$ 30,000	Ken, Capital	$ 30,000
		Total Liabilities and	
Total Assets	$100,000	Partners' Capital	$100,000

The partners agree to receive their cash at the end of the liquidation process. During the liquidation process, the partnership:

- collects $30,000 of the receivables
- sells the equipment for $10,000.
- pays the partnership debts.

Required:

Compute the amount of cash each partner receives.

Exercise 2-9

Liquidation Plan (LO 5)

Gary and Bette are partners with the following balance sheet:

Cash	$30,000	Accounts Payable	$20,000
Building	$40,000	Notes Payable, Gary	$30,000
		Gary, Capital	$10,000
		Bette, Capital	$10,000
		Total Liabilities and	
Total Assets	$70,000	Partners' Capital	$70,000

During their liquidation process, the following transactions occur:

- The building is sold for $60,000.
- Partnership Liabilities are paid.
- Liquidation expenses were $10,000.

Required:

Compute the amount of cash each partner receives.

Exercise 2-10

Lump-Sum Liquidation: Partner with Debit Balance (LO 4)

Stephen and Adam are equal partners who decide to liquidate with the following balance sheet:

Cash	$30,000	Accounts Payable	$30,000
Accounts Receivable, Adam	$10,000	Notes Payable, Stephen	$20,000
Equipment	$50,000	Stephen, Capital	$25,000
		Adam, Capital	$15,000
		Total Liabilities and	
Total Assets	$90,000	Partners' Capital	$90,000

During their liquidation process, the following transactions occur:

- The equipment is sold for $40,000.
- Partnership Liabilities are paid.
- Liquidation expenses were $20,000.

Required:

Compute the amount of cash each partner receives, assuming both partners have sufficient personal assets to cover any liabilities to the partnership.

Exercise 2-11

Liquidation Plan (LO 4 & 5)

Barney and Smith share profits and losses 25%/75%. They have decided to liquidate their partnership when the partnership had the following balance sheet:

Cash	$ 30,000	Accounts Payable	$ 25,000
Accounts Receivable	$ 60,000	Barney, Capital	$ 75,000
Building	$ 50,000	Smith, Capital	$ 40,000
		Total Liabilities and	
Total Assets	$110,000	Partners' Capital	$110,000

The partnership collected $20,000 of their receivables. The rest of the process will take a few months, and Barney wanted some of his cash. How much cash can Barney receive at this time?

Exercise 2-12

Liquidation Plan (LO 4 & 5)

Sandra and Richard are partners with a 6/4 profit ratio when they decide to liquidate their partnership with the following balance sheet:

Cash	$50,000	Accounts Payable	$30,000
Land	$40,000	Notes Payable, Sandra	$15,000
		Sandra, Capital	$25,000
		Richard, Capital	$20,000
		Total Liabilities and	
Total Assets	$90,000	Partners' Capital	$90,000

The process will take at least six months, and the partners want their cash as soon as possible. They estimate that there will be liquidation expenses of $15,000. How much cash can be paid to the partners immediately?

Exercise 2-13

Liquidation Plan: Non-Equal Profit-Sharing Ratio (LO 4 & 5)

Peter, Paul, and Mary share profits in their partnership as 30/30/40, respectively. They have decided to liquidate their partnership. Their attorney told them his fees would be $10,000 to process the liquidation. If the partnership has the following balance sheet, how much cash can each partner receive immediately?

Cash	$ 50,000	Accounts Payable	$ 10,000
Accounts Receivable, Mary	$ 10,000	Notes Payable, Peter	$ 20,000
Accounts Receivable, Net	$ 40,000	Peter, Capital	$ 30,000
Land	$ 20,000	Paul, Capital	$ 30,000
		Mary, Capital	$ 30,000
		Total Liabilities and	
Total Assets	$120,000	Partners' Capital	$120,000

PROBLEMS

Problem 2-1

Partner Withdrawal (LO 1 & 2)

Johnson, Keller, and Lee have a partnership with the following balance sheet:

Cash	$ 50,000	Liabilities	$ 20,000
Investments	$ 40,000	Johnson, Capital	$ 50,000
Other Assets	$120,000	Keller, Capital	$ 60,000
		Lee, Capital	$ 80,000
		Total Liabilities and	
Total Assets	$210,000	Partners' Capital	$210,000

Johnson, Keller, and Lee have a 30%/30%/40% profit-sharing ratio, respectively. Lee wants to leave the partnership. Johnson and Keller are discussing three ways to acquire Lee's interest:

1. Use their personal assets.
2. Provide Lee with a Note that promises a portion of future earnings.
3. Sell $30,000 of their investments for $70,000 and then use cash from the partnership.

Required:

   a. Write a memo discussing the advantages and disadvantages to all of the partners for each of these methods of acquiring Lee's interest.
   b. Johnson and Keller decide the best method is to sell their investments. Provide the journal entries to be recorded by the partnership.

Problem 2-2

Partner Withdrawal: Comparison of Bonus and Goodwill Methods (LO 1)

Bill, Gary, and Al are partners who have a 4/3/3 profit ratio with the following balance sheet:

Cash	$100,000	Liabilities	$ 50,000
Other Assets	$200,000	Bill, Capital	$ 80,000
		Gary, Capital	$100,000
		Al, Capital	$ 70,000
		Total Liabilities and	
Total Assets	$300,000	Partners' Capital	$300,000

Bill and Gary want to acquire Al's interest for $98,000.

Required:

Prepare the partnership journal entries for each of the following independent situations:
  a. The partnership uses the bonus method when partners are admitted or withdraw.
  b. The partnership uses the goodwill method to only value the share of the withdrawing partner.
  c. The partnership uses the goodwill method where the total partnership is revalued when a partner withdraws.

Problem 2-3

Death of Partner: Comparison of Various Methods (LO 1)

Samson, Goliath, and Delilah are 40/40/20 partners with capital balances of $80,000, $70,000, and $30,000, respectively. Samson dies.

Required:

Prepare the partnership journal entries for each of the following independent situations.
  a. The partnership pays Samson's estate $50,000 for his interest.
  b. The partnership pays Samson's estate $104,000. The partnership uses the bonus method.
  c. The partnership pays Samson's estate $104,000. The partnership uses the goodwill method.

Problem 2-4

Liquidation Journal Entries: Lump-Sum (LO 3)

Jen, Steve, and Sue are partners. On January 31, they decide to liquidate their partnership with the following balance sheet:

Cash	$30,000	Accounts Payable	$17,000
Accounts Receivable	$42,000	Jen, Capital	$30,000
Land	$20,000	Steve, Capital	$25,000
		Sue, Capital	$20,000
		Total Liabilities and	
Total Assets	$92,000	Partners' Capital	$92,000

During the liquidation process, the following events occurred:
  Feb. 1   Sold the land for $50,000.
  Feb. 1   Paid Liabilities.
  Feb. 21   Collected Accounts Receivable.
  Feb. 28   Distributed Cash to partners.

Required:

Prepare all partnership entries for the month of February.

Problem 2-5

Liquidation Plan: Partners May Be Insolvent (LO 3 & 5)

Rob, Sharon, and Dave share profits 30/30/40. On February 28, the partnership had the following balance sheet:

Cash	$ 20,000	Accounts Payable	$ 30,000
Accounts Receivable	$ 50,000	Rob, Capital	$ 30,000
Supplies	$ 25,000	Sharon, Capital	$ 30,000
Land	$ 5,000	Dave, Capital	$ 10,000
		Total Liabilities and	
Total Assets	$100,000	Partners' Capital	$100,000

During March, they decided to liquidate, and the following events occurred:

March 15 Sold land for $15,000.
March 15 Collected $25,000 from the accounts receivable. The remaining receivables are deemed uncollectible.
March 31 Sold supplies for $10,000.
March 31 Paid Liabilities.
April 1   Distributed Cash to the partners.

Required:

a. Prepare a lump-sum liquidation plan as of April 1. Assume all partners are solvent and can repay any debts to the partnership on April 1.
b. Prepare a lump-sum liquidation plan as of April 1. Assume partners are not individually solvent and cannot repay any partnership debts on April 1.
c. Prepare the partnership journal entries for Requirement a.
d. Prepare the partnership journal entry for Requirement b, April 1 only.

Problem 2-6

Liquidation Journal Entries: Installment Method (Exercise 4 as Installment) (LO 3)

Jen, Steve, and Sue are partners. They decide to liquidate their partnership with the following balance sheet:

Cash	$30,000	Accounts Payable	$17,000
Accounts Receivable	$42,000	Jen, Capital	$30,000
Land	$20,000	Steve, Capital	$25,000
		Sue, Capital	$20,000
		Total Liabilities and	
Total Assets	$92,000	Partners' Capital	$92,000

During the liquidation process, the following events occurred:

Feb. 1   Sold the land for $50,000.
Feb. 1   Paid Liabilities.
Feb. 1   Distributed Cash to partners.
Feb. 21 Collected Accounts Receivable.
Feb. 28 Distributed Cash to partners.

Required:

Prepare all partnership entries for the month of February.

Problem 2-7

Installment Liquidation Plan and Journal Entries: Non-Equal Profit-Sharing Ratio (LO 3 & 5)

Rob, Sharon, and Dave share profits 30/30/40. On February 28, the partnership had the following balance sheet:

Cash	$ 20,000	Accounts Payable	$ 30,000
Accounts Receivable	$ 50,000	Rob, Capital	$ 30,000
Supplies	$ 25,000	Sharon, Capital	$ 30,000
Land	$ 5,000	Dave, Capital	$ 10,000
		Total Liabilities and	
Total Assets	$100,000	Partners' Capital	$100,000

During March, they decided to liquidate, and the following events occurred:

March 15	Sold land for $15,000.
March 15	Collected $25,000 from the accounts receivable. The remaining receivables are deemed uncollectible.
March 15	Paid Liabilities.
March 15	Distributed Cash to partners.
March 31	Sold supplies for $10,000.
April 1	Distributed Cash to partners.

Required:

    a. Prepare an installment liquidation plan as of March 15.

    b. Prepare the partnership journal entries for April 1, assuming the partners are solvent and can repay any debts to the partnership.

    c. Prepare the partnership journal entries for April, assuming the partners are not individually solvent and cannot repay any partnership debts.

Problem 2-8

Installment Liquidation Plan (LO 3 & 5)

Marsha, Martha, and Marion are partners. They decide to liquidate their partnership with the following May 31 balance sheet:

Cash	$ 50,000	Accounts Payable	$ 30,000
Accounts Receivable	$ 70,000	Marsha, Capital	$ 60,000
Equipment	$ 50,000	Martha, Capital	$ 40,000
		Marion, Capital	$ 40,000
		Total Liabilities and	
Total Assets	$170,000	Partners' Capital	$170,000

During the liquidation process, the following events occurred:

June 1	Collected $30,000 of receivables.
June 1	Distributed available Cash to partners.
June 5	Paid partnership Liabilities.
June 8	Collected $10,000 of receivables. The remaining receivables are deemed uncollectible.
June 19	Sold equipment for $11,000.
June 20	Distributed available Cash to partners.

Required:

    a. Determine the amount of Cash distributed to each partner on June 1.

    b. Determine the amount of Cash distributed to each partner on June 20.

Problem 2-9

Explain Installment Liquidation Process (LO 3 & 5)

Marsha, Martha, and Marian are partners. They decide to liquidate the partnership with the following May 31 balance sheet:

Cash	$ 50,000	Accounts Payable	$ 30,000
Accounts Receivable	$ 70,000	Marsha, Capital	$ 60,000
Equipment	$ 50,000	Martha, Capital	$ 40,000
		Marian, Capital	$ 40,000
		Total Liabilities and	
Total Assets	$170,000	Partners' Capital	$170,000

The partners agree to liquidate the partnership. They each want as much cash as possible, as soon as possible.

Required:

Write a memo to the partners explaining how much cash can be distributed immediately. Include in the memo your recommendation as to how and when the cash should be distributed.

Problem 2-10

Installment Liquidation Process (LO 3 & 5)

Harvey, Harry, and Hope are partners. They decide to liquidate their partnership on August 1 with the following balance sheet:

Cash	$ 60,000	Accounts Payable	$ 40,000
Accounts Receivable, Harry	$ 20,000	Notes Payable, Harvey	$ 10,000
Accounts Receivable	$ 80,000	Harvey, Capital	$ 40,000
Equipment	$ 70,000	Hope, Capital	$ 65,000
		Harry, Capital	$ 75,000
		Total Liabilities and	
Total Assets	$230,000	Partners' Capital	$230,000

The partners want to be able to distribute cash as soon as it is available. During the liquidation process, the following events occurred:

August 1	Distributed available Cash to partners.
August 8	Paid partnership debts.
August 10	Collected $60,000 of Accounts Receivable.
August 11	Distributed available Cash to partners.
August 15	Sold equipment for $55,000.
August 16	Collected $11,000 of receivables. The remaining balance is deemed uncollectible.
August 17	Distributed available Cash.

Required:

a. Determine the amount of cash distributed to each partner on August 1.
b. Determine the amount of cash distributed on August 11.
c. Determine the amount of cash distributed on August 17.

Problem 2-11

Installment Liquidation Process with Cash Contingency (LO 3 & 5)

Harvey, Harry, and Hope are partners. They decide to liquidate their partnership on August 1 with the following balance sheet:

Cash	$ 60,000	Accounts Payable	$ 40,000
Accounts Receivable, Harry	$ 20,000	Notes Payable, Harvey	$ 10,000
Accounts Receivable	$ 80,000	Harvey, Capital	$ 40,000
Equipment	$ 70,000	Hope, Capital	$ 65,000
		Harry, Capital	$ 75,000
		Total Liabilities and	
Total Assets	$230,000	Partners' Capital	$230,000

During the liquidation process, they anticipate the need for $6,000 of cash that will be held in contingency and the following events occurred:

August 1   Distributed available Cash to partners.
August 8   Paid partnership debts.
August 10 Collected $60,000 of Accounts Receivable.
August 11 Distributed available Cash to partners.
August 15 Sold equipment for $55,000.
August 16 Collected $11,000 of receivables. The remaining balance is deemed uncollectible.
August 17 Distributed available Cash.

Required:

a. Determine the amount of cash distributed to each partner on August 1.
b. Determine the amount of cash distributed on August 11.
c. Determine the amount of cash distributed on August 17.

Problem 2-12

Installment Liquidation with Journal Entries (LO 3 & 5)

Maple, Oak, and Pine decide to liquidate their partnership on September 1 when the partnership had the following balance sheet:

Cash	$ 90,000	Accounts Payable	$ 50,000
Accounts Receivable	$ 80,000	Maple, Capital	$ 95,000
Supplies	$ 60,000	Oak, Capital	$ 35,000
		Pine, Capital	$ 50,000
		Total Liabilities and	
Total Assets	$230,000	Partners' Capital	$230,000

The partners have a 5/2/3 profit-sharing ratio for Maple, Oak, and Pine, respectively. The partners agreed to maintain a $20,000 contingency during the liquidation. The following events occurred during the liquidation process:

September 1   Distributed available Cash to the partners.
September 10 Paid Liabilities.
September 13 Collected $30,000 of receivables. The remaining receivables were deemed uncollectible.
September 20 Sold supplies for $40,000.
September 22 Paid $15,000 of liquidation expenses.
September 22 Distributed available Cash to partners.

Required:

a. Prepare the partnership journal entry for September 1. Develop a schedule in support of the journal entry.
b. Determine the amount of cash distributed to each partner on September 22.

Problem 2-13

Installment Liquidation: Insolvent Partner (LO 3, 4, & 5)

Apple, Cherry, and Peach decided to liquidate their partnership on September 1 when the partnership had the following balance sheet:

Cash	$ 90,000	Accounts Payable	$ 50,000
Accounts Receivable	$ 80,000	Apple, Capital	$ 95,000
Supplies	$ 60,000	Cherry, Capital	$ 35,000
		Peach, Capital	$ 50,000
		Total Liabilities and	
Total Assets	$230,000	Partners' Capital	$230,000

The partners have a 3/5/2 profit-sharing ratio for Apple, Cherry, and Peach, respectively. The partners agreed to maintain a $20,000 contingency during the liquidation. The partners are individually solvent and have agreed to repay any capital deficiencies. The following events occurred during the liquidation process:

September 1	Distributed available Cash to the partners.
September 10	Paid Liabilities.
September 13	Collected $30,000 of receivables. The remaining receivables were deemed uncollectible.
September 20	Sold supplies for $40,000.
September 22	Paid $15,000 of liquidation expenses.
September 22	Distributed available Cash to partners.

Required:

   a. Prepare the partnership journal entry for September 1. Develop schedule in support of the journal entry.
   b. Determine the amount of cash distributed to each partner on September 22.

Problem 2-14

CASE: Explain Installment Liquidation Process (LO 3, 4, & 5)

Spring, Winter, and Fall are partners who have the following personal assets (assume all are liquid) and personal liabilities:

	Personal Assets	**Personal Liabilities**
Spring	60,000	90,000
Winter	40,000	20,000
Fall	40,000	60,000

They have decided to liquidate their business in which they have a 3/3/4 profit-sharing ratio. At the point of liquidation, the partnership balance sheet contained the following accounts:

Cash	20,000	Accounts Payable	40,000
Accounts Receivable	80,000	Spring, Capital	70,000
Supplies	50,000	Winter, Capital	20,000
		Fall, Capital	20,000
		Total Liabilities and	
Total Assets	150,000	Partners' Capital	150,000

During the liquidation, the receivables were found to be uncollectible and the supplies were sold for $15,000.

Required:

   a. How much cash was paid to partnership creditors?
   b. How much cash did each partner have to contribute to the partnership?
   c. How much cash will personal creditors receive from personal assets and the distribution from the partnership?
   d. Write a memo to Ms. Spring explaining why she did not receive as much from the partnership as she expected.

Problem 2-15

CASE: Explain Installment Liquidation Process (LO 3, 4, & 5)

Larry, Curley, and Moe are partners who all have the same capital balance. Their balance sheet currently consists of:

Cash	40,000
Accounts Receivable	80,000
Land	20,000
Accounts Payable	50,000

The partners believe they can collect on the receivables:

Within 30 days	25,000
Within 60 days	30,000
Within 90 days	6,000
Unsure if collectible	19,000

They have an option to sell the land in 90 days for $60,000. Curley has been approached by a real estate agent who is encouraging the partners to wait six months before selling the property because then they should be able to sell it for $90,000.

Larry wants the partnership to distribute the $40,000 now.

Required:

Write a memo to the partners explaining when cash can be distributed to the partners over the next 3 months. Prepare supporting schedules.

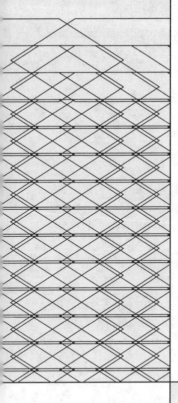

CHAPTER 3

TAXATION ISSUES ASSOCIATED WITH PARTNERSHIPS

LEARNING OBJECTIVES

- Explain how tax laws define partners and partnerships.
- Discuss tax consequences of the formation of a partnership.
- Compute a partner's tax basis.
- Compute a partner's share of income or loss items.
- Explain the tax impact of a partnership distribution.
- Compute partnership income or loss.

In Chapter 1, April and Leo formed a partnership and added Sheri as a partner. That discussion centered on the impact on the partnership and the accounting entries in support of the transaction. For ease in understanding the concepts, cash was the asset contributed or distributed.

That discussion also excluded tax consequences of the decisions. Accounting for the tax implications of the relationship between the individual partners and the partnership changes when assets other than cash are contributed or distributed. This chapter will provide an overview of some of the major issues in partnership taxation. The issues can become very complex, and the actual tax law and accompanying regulations need to be referenced prior to providing actual advice to a client.

This chapter contains an introduction to the various forms of pass-through entities, a discussion of definitions, and of some of the different tax-related issues. It concludes with an example of completing a partnership tax-return Form 1065. Tax forms, instructions, and IRS publications can be located on and downloaded from the IRS website http://www.irs.gov/. Another site with information about partnership tax issues is http://www.1065accountant.com. References to the 1986 Internal Revenue Code sections will be based upon using "IRC" and then applicable section number.

TAX DEFINITION OF A PARTNERSHIP (LO 1)

An advantage of a partnership is that it is not subject to income tax. However, the individual partners carrying on the business are separately liable for income taxes (IRC 701). The partnership is required to file an information tax return, Form 1065, that allocates the income to the individual partners. A partnership thus has the advantage to "pass through" its income to the individual partners. Then, each of the partners will report his/her share of this reported income.

The tax code defines a **partnership** as an unincorporated organization. A partnership may include a syndicate, group, or joint venture; however, it cannot be one individual. A **partner** is a member of a partnership. The tax code also allows for the existence of a **partnership agreement** to determine a partner's distributive share of income. A **liquidation of a partner's interest** is defined as a termination of the partner's entire interest. (Section 761, 1986 IRS Code.)

Limited liability partnership (LLP) and **limited liability corporation (LLC)** are legal forms of organization that have been allowed by most states and the IRS. These forms of organization allow most entities to have the possibility to enjoy the pass-through benefits of a partnership and the limited liability protection of a corporation.

An LLC, with two or more members, will automatically be classified as a partnership. A single-person LLC will be treated for tax purposes the same as a sole-proprietorship. An LLC can, however, elect to be treated as a corporation for federal tax purposes. Other unincorporated entities can choose to be treated as either a partnership or a corporation for tax purposes under what is referred to as **check-the-box regulations** by completing Form 8832, Entity Classification Election (Regulation 301.7701).

LLPs aid professional practices—such as those of accountants, attorneys, and physicians—to minimize the liability of individual partners from the malpractice of the other partners. An LLP is treated as a partnership in all other respects. Generally, if *A&L* had been formed as an LLP, then April would be responsible for her individual malpractice but not for the professional malpractice of her other partners, Leo and Sheri.

A **family partnership** can be used to reduce taxes by splitting income among family members where **capital is a material income-producing factor** (Section 704, 1986 IRS Code). Due to the income-splitting features, a family partnership is a common form of estate-planning vehicle. It must be noted that the partnership must have a valid business purpose.

The tax regulations specify that the intent of the law is to provide taxpayers with the ability to transact business in a flexible manner without being taxed at the entity level. The regulations assume that the intent of the partnership and the partners is to not pay entity-level taxes and, therefore, provide these three requirements:

- the partnership will operate for a bona fide business purpose;
- the form of the transaction must be respected in substance over form requirements;
- transactions between the partner and the partnership must reflect the partner's economic agreement and clearly reflect the partner's income.

Should these requirements not be fulfilled, the regulations provide the Commissioner of the Internal Revenue Service with the power to recast partnership transactions.

◤ CONCEPTUAL QUESTION AND REFLECTION

John Jones is 45% owner of JJ Inc. He would like to form an alliance with JJ Inc. where he receives 50% of the profits and JJ Inc. receives the rest. As his CPA, would you agree with the formation of this alliance?

TAX DECISIONS MADE AT THE PARTNERSHIP LEVEL (LO 2)

The partnership is not a taxable entity. However, certain elections made at the partnership level must be followed by the individual partners. For instance, the partnership selects an accounting method. Other partnership-level issues include:

- depreciation methods,
- capitalizing or expensing qualified business expenses,
- basis adjustment of certain partnership property, and
- tax audits.

The impact of these various decisions will be discussed in more detail.

Accounting Methods

A partner's share of profits and losses is based upon the accounting method used by the partnership. The differences between the cash basis and accrual basis of accounting were discussed in Chapter 1. Using the cash basis, revenue and expenses are recognized when cash is received or paid. Typically, individual partners use a cash basis. It is possible then to have an accrual basis partnership and a cash basis partner. Under this situation, the partner would include income allocations based upon partnership accrual computations (i.e., cash has not been received nor paid).

CASH OR ACCRUAL BASIS: THE IMPACT OF IRS REVENUE PROCEDURES 2000-22 AND 2001-10

Small business owners know how to run their businesses but are often plagued by having to maintain records using accounting procedures they do not understand. The IRS in Revenue Procedure 2000-22 allows entities regardless of structure, such as sole-proprietorships, partnerships, S-corporations, and regular C-corporations, to use the cash basis of accounting if the entity meets the **sales test**. The sales test requires that revenues, on average, over the prior three years are $1 million or less. In the past, entities that sold merchandise as a material-income producing factor had to use the accrual basis regardless of gross revenue.

Revenue Procedure 2001-10 modified Revenue Procedure 2000-22. Businesses must maintain adequate books and records. However, the accounting method used in keeping the accounts is not specified.

The revenue procedures are available online at www.revenueprocedures.com. Further information related to the impact of these revenue procedures can be found by reading "Cash or Accrual?" written by Robert Jennings, CPA, in the May 2001 *Journal of Accountancy*, pp. 37 – 39.

CAPITALIZING OR EXPENSING QUALIFIED BUSINESS EXPENSES

Generally, there is no deduction allowed to a partnership for any amounts paid or incurred to organize a partnership. These non-deductible expenses include syndication fees paid to organize or promote the sale of an interest in the partnership.

The partnership may, however, elect to capitalize organization expenses. **Organization costs** associated with forming the partnership, such as accounting and legal fees, and **start-up costs** for beginning the business, such as marketing research surveys, can be amortized ratably even though those expenses would normally benefit the partnership throughout its entire life. These deferred expenses can then be amortized over a period of not less than 60 months (IRC 709).

Organization and start-up costs need to be differentiated from **syndication costs**. Syndication costs are associated with selling and marketing partnership units to prospective new partners. These costs—which may include brokerage, legal, and accounting fees—are to be capitalized but are not to be amortized for tax purposes.

Tax Audits

Individual partners are responsible for reporting for tax purposes. However, the IRS audits partnership items, where the detail is available, at the partnership level. The IRS will deal with one partner on behalf of all of the partners. All partnerships subject to consolidated audit reports must designate a general partner as the **tax matters partner** for dealing with the partnership audit. Any discrepancies found at the partnership level are reported to the individual partners. Amended individual tax returns are then filed.

Taxable Year

A partnership determines its taxable year based upon applying a set of complex technical rules. The taxable year of the principal partner is an important consideration in this decision. While there is some flexibility, the partnership does not have the absolute authority to determine its own tax year.

This decision regarding the taxable year of the partnership is important because the partner must report his or her share of the distributive items for any partnership that has a taxable year-end within the partner's taxable year. The partner must also include in income **guaranteed payments** that are made to him or her in a partnership taxable year ending with or during the partner's taxable year. Guaranteed payments are determined without regard to the income of the partnership and are discussed further within the section titled **Transactions Between Partnership and Partners**.

A new partnership can establish the taxable year as a calendar year, or it can be the same as all of its principal partners. Options other than these require IRS approval that is based upon a variety of tests related to the majority interest taxable year (IRC 706).

BASIS: PARTNERS AND PARTNERSHIP (LO 3)

In Chapter 1, a partner's contribution to the partnership was determined based upon the fair market value of the asset contributed. The amount contributed then became the partner's capital balance. While this is true for accounting purposes, there is a difference for tax purposes. The contribution of assets to a partnership is not considered to be a taxable event at the time of the contribution. Therefore, if a partner pays $10,000 for a piece of property and contributes it to a partnership when the fair market value is $25,000, neither the partner nor the partnership records income and no taxes are paid. However, the partner really only contributed an asset that cost him or her $10,000. This $10,000 is the partner's basis for tax purposes with the recognition of any potential gain being deferred. What follows is a discussion of some rules and situations related to this complicated subject.

Contributing Assets at Fair Market Value

In Chapter 1, April and Leo contributed the following to *A&L* when they originally formed their partnership:

	April	Leo
Computer	$10,000	$ 5,000
Cash	$10,000	$ 5,000
	$20,000	$10,000

Each of them owned the assets contributed. The computer systems were new when they were contributed. In this situation, April and Leo each contributed assets with a cost that was equivalent to the asset's fair market value. April's and Leo's basis in the assets contributed was $20,000 and $10,000, respectively, which equaled the fair market values when contributed.

Contributing Assets Other than Cash

In Chapter 1, when Sheri was admitted to the partnership, she was assumed to contribute $20,000 in cash. Instead, she could have contributed other assets such as marketable securities. Assume that she had acquired the securities for $10,000 and that the day they were contributed to the partnership the securities had a fair market value of $20,000. In this case, the partnership entries would have been valued the same as if the partnership had received cash.

Marketable Securities	$20,000	
Sheri, Capital		$20,000

Sheri's Capital account on the partnership books would have been $20,000. However, for tax purposes Sheri would have a tax basis of $10,000, the amount originally paid for the securities.

Contributing assets to form or join a partnership is not considered to be a taxable event as the recognition of any gain is being deferred (IRC 721). The basis to the partner is the partner's adjusted basis at the time of the contribution (IRC 722). In the example above, Sheri's tax basis is $10,000. If the partnership, *A&L*, should immediately distribute the property to Leo, then *A&L*'s substitute tax basis is also Sheri's adjusted tax basis, again in this case $10,000 (IRC 723). The $10,000 gain is passed through to Sheri who is subject to paying the appropriate income tax.

The accounting valuation and the tax valuation can be different. The tax advisors to the individual partners and the partnership must be aware of the existence of the different valuations of the individual partner's basis.

EXCEPTIONS TO NON-RECOGNITION OF INCOME UPON FORMATION OF A PARTNERSHIP

Regulation 1.721 provides exceptions to IRC 721. Income can be recognized upon formation of a partnership if the transaction is a(n):

- taxable exchange of properties;
- disguised sale of properties;
- exchange of services rendered in exchange for a capital interest;
- contribution of appreciated stock to an investment partnership.

Impact on a Partner's Tax Basis for an Increase in Partnership Liabilities

A partner that assumes a liability for the partnership is treated as if a contribution has been made and his or her basis in the partnership increases. This increase in basis can be the result of the partnership debt increasing or by the partnership itself assuming a liability from a partner. For example, assume that the A&B partnership incurred more liabilities than were paid during the year and for this example there was no income.

	Beginning of the Year	End of the Year
Assets	$30,000	$40,000
Liabilities	$10,000	$20,000
A, Capital (60%)	$12,000	$12,000
B, Capital (40%)	$ 8,000	$ 8,000
Tax Basis:		
A	$18,000	$24,000
B	$12,000	$16,000

Each partner's tax basis increased by his or her individual profit-sharing ratio times the $10,000 increase of liabilities. Therefore, A's basis and B's basis increase $6,000 and $4,000, respectively.

Contributing Assets with a Liability

In the case of the partnership assuming the liability of a partner, the partner is treated as if the partnership gave the partner money in payment of the liability. The partner's capital interest is therefore reduced to the extent of the other partners' income-sharing percentage.

Let's assume that Chris has also joined the *A&L* partnership at a time when the partnership had no liabilities. His capital contribution to the partnership, for a 10% interest, included a building, which had been used for income-producing purposes, that has a fair market value of $100,000 with a $70,000 mortgage. He had originally purchased the building for $80,000. Upon contributing the asset to the partnership, the partnership assumed the mortgage. This transaction resulted in Chris having a $30,000 Capital account balance, but a $17,000 tax basis.

Chris's adjusted basis of property contributed:	$80,000
Less: portion of mortgage assumed by other partners 90% * 70,000:	(63,000)
Chris's tax basis	$17,000

It can be seen, then, that the tax code treats the assumption of a mortgage by the partnership the same as a distribution of money to the contributing partner. Due to the partnership assuming the mortgage, the tax code also treats the other partners as if they have increased their basis by making a contribution.

ILLUSTRATION OF PARTNER CONTRIBUTING DEBT WHEN THE PARTNERSHIP HAS EXISTING DEBT

The example just discussed assumes that *A&L* had no liabilities when Chris joined the partnership. If the partnership had $10,000 of liabilities, then Chris's tax basis would be $18,000:

Chris's adjusted basis of property contributed:	$80,000
Less: portion of mortgage assumed by other partners 90% * 70,000	(63,000)
Plus: portion of existing liabilities assumed by Chris 10% * 10,000	1,000
Chris's tax basis	$18,000

This example treats the mortgage as **recourse debt**. Recourse debt is partnership debt for which at least one if not all of the partners are considered to be personally liable. This liability can be a matter of law or as a result of personal guarantees. In this text, the attribution of recourse debt will be based upon each partner's profit- and loss-sharing ratio. This is a simplification of the recourse debt rules, which require the debt to be shared based upon an implied liquidation scenario that is beyond the scope of this text.

There is an exception to not recognizing income upon forming a partnership. A partner's basis in a partnership can never be less than $0. If Chris had originally purchased the contributed building for $50,000, then his basis as calculated above would be ($13,000).

Chris's adjusted basis of property contributed:	$50,000
Less: portion of mortgage assumed by other	
Partners 90% * 70,000:	(63,000)
Chris's tax basis	($13,000)

In this situation, the assumption of the mortgage is treated as a cash distribution and Chris must recognize a capital gain of $13,000 upon forming the partnership. This is, in effect, an increase in Chris's adjusted basis so that his tax basis is then $0.

This discussion ignores the implications of **non-recourse debt**. Non-recourse debt is partnership debt for which no person will be held personally liable. The regulations discussing IRC 704 provide further information concerning the lack of substantial economic effect associated with non-recourse debt. Non-recourse debt is a complicating factor that is beyond the scope of this text.

● **INTERPRETIVE EXERCISE**

Assume that Chris contributed a building that he acquired for $90,000 with a $110,000 fair market value for a 20% interest in the partnership. The partnership assumes a $60,000 mortgage associated with the building. What are Chris's capital account balance and tax basis?

Continuing Computation of the Basis

The above discussion explained how a partner's original basis is computed. After the original contribution, a partner's basis in the partnership will be adjusted every year. The determination of a partner's basis will be increased or decreased for transactions occurring during the year. IRC sections 705, 722, 742, and 752 define how to determine a partner's adjusted basis. Examples of items increasing the basis based upon the IRC are:

■ new contributions (IRC 722);
■ share of profits on taxable income;
■ share of profits on non-taxable income;
■ liabilities of other partners assumed by the partnership;
■ increase in a partner's share of partnership liabilities.

An individual partner's basis can never be decreased below zero ($0). Examples of items decreasing a partner's basis are:

■ distributions to the partner,
■ share of losses,
■ share of expenditures not properly included in the computation of taxable income and not properly chargeable to the capital account,
■ contributed liabilities assumed by the partnership,
■ decrease in partner's share of partnership liabilities.

An interesting aspect associated with accounting for partnerships and partners is the impact of liabilities. An increase in partnership liabilities results in an increase in the individual partner's basis, whereas a decrease in partnership liabilities causes a decrease in the individual partner's basis. For example, with the *A&L* partnership, the three partners (April, Leo, and Sheri) have a profit-sharing ratio of 40%/40%/20%.

If at the end of the year the partnership had outstanding liabilities such as an account payable for electricity of $1,000, then the individual basis of each of the three partners would increase $400, $400, and $200, respectively.

A partnership interest includes both an interest in capital as well as an interest in future profits. An interest in future profits includes an interest in the appreciation of the underlying partnership assets. Economically, this can be seen as an issue for partners with a profit interest as well as those with a capital interest in the partnership.

An individual such as an accountant or attorney may be offered a share in a partnership in exchange for personal services rendered. As mentioned earlier, the receipt of the partnership capital interest is treated as taxable income. This is noted above as an exception to the non-recognition provision of IRC 721. The amount of the income is based upon the fair market value of the transferred interest. The valuation of the transferred interest, while necessary, is difficult to compute because future profits can be a function of both return on assets and appreciation of assets.

Valuing partner interests or valuing a business is an interesting and challenging career path for accountants. The American Institute of Certified Public Accountants has a separate Accredited in Business Valuation (ABV) designation. This designation recognizes CPAs with additional education and experience in business valuation.

For more information on valuing partnership interests transferred for services, see: "Receipt of Partnership Interest in Exchange for Services: Still Polishing the Diamond," by Lori S. Hoberman, *Journal of Partnership Taxation*, pp. 336 – 353.

Special Handling of Pre-Contribution Gain or Loss Section 704(c) Property

Andy and Harry are equal partners in A&H. When forming the partnership, Andy contributed $15,000 in cash. Harry contributed land with an adjusted tax basis of $5,000 and a fair market value of $15,000. At the time of contribution, Harry has a potential built-in gain of $10,000. Harry never recognized as income the excess of the property's fair market value ($15,000) over his adjusted basis ($5,000) since during the formation of the partnership the contribution is not a taxable event, even though Harry's capital interest reflected the higher amount (the fair market value of $15,000).

The purpose of IRC 704(c) is to prevent the shifting of tax benefits among partners for a precontribution gain or loss. Assume that after forming the partnership, the property was sold for $15,000. The partnership would realize a gain for tax purposes of $10,000 (partnership book value $15,000 – partnership tax basis). This gain must be allocated entirely to Harry. In this manner, the precontribution gain has been realized and is being recognized by Harry prior to any gain being allocated to the other partners.

If instead of selling the land for $15,000 the partnership sold the land for $21,000, then there would be a realized tax gain of $16,000 ($21,000 – $5,000). In this case, $10,000 plus half of the remainder will be allocated to Harry.

	Total	Harry	Andy
Realized Gain	$16,000		
Built-in Gain	$10,000	$10,000	
To be split	$ 6,000	$ 3,000	$3,000
Gain taxable to each partner		$13,000	$3,000

Should the property be sold for less than $15,000, then the total gain would be allocated to Harry. In this manner, Harry is not able to shift income to other partners by contributing an appreciated asset to the partnership.

EXPLANATION OF IMPACT OF PRECONTRIBUTION GAIN WITH DEPRECIABLE PROPERTY

In the discussion of precontribution gain above, Harry contributed land. The use of land as the example was to aid in the understanding of a difficult concept. Property other than land gets even more complicated with the impact of depreciation. The following example includes depreciation; however, it is simplified for both book and tax purposes to assume that the partnership has elected to use straight-line depreciation and for ease in understanding a 10-year useful life. This is simplified because tax depreciation is based upon the Modified Accelerated Cost Recovery System (MACRS) that assumes accelerated depreciation and does not use a 10-year useful life. The purpose of this example is to provide a glimpse into some of the complexities of partnership accounting and tax reporting.

John and Sally are equal partners in J&S. When forming the partnership, John contributed $20,000 in cash. Sally contributed property with a 10-year useful life, having an adjusted tax basis of $8,000 and a fair market value of $20,000. Sally has a potential built-in gain of $12,000, the excess of the property's fair market value ($20,000) over her adjusted basis ($8,000). The partnership will use as a book value the $20,000 fair market value of the contribution.

To prevent shifting of tax benefits in accordance with IRC 704(c), there must be a separate depreciation computation for both book and tax purposes. Assuming straight-line depreciation, this results in annual depreciation of $2,000 (book) and $800 (tax). The partnership is only able to allocate $800 ($8,000/10) on the tax return. Since John is entitled to receive up to $1,000 (50% * $2,000), the regulations [1.704-3(b)(2)(ii)] specify that the total tax depreciation be allocated to him.

During the first year, assume there are no other expenses or income generated by the partnership. Each partner's capital account balance is $19,000 ($20,000 Beginning Balance less $1,000 (50% of $2,000 of Book Depreciation Expense). John's basis is $19,200 ($20,000 Beginning Balance less $800 of Tax Depreciation). Sally's tax basis is unchanged. The individual partner's basis and the partnership basis can be summarized as:

	John	Sally
Capital Account	$19,000	$19,000
Basis	$19,200	$ 8,000

The partnership has an asset with a(n):

book value of ($20,000 – $2,000)	$18,000
adjusted tax basis of ($8,000 – $800)	$ 7,200
remaining built-in gain	$10,800

At this time, Sally's built-in gain with respect to the property decreases to $10,800.

Assume at the beginning of the second year the property is sold for $18,000. The partnership realizes a tax gain of $10,800 (book value of $18,000 – adjusted tax basis of $7,200). This gain must be allocated entirely to Sally.

(continued on next page)

If instead the property were sold for $21,200, then there would be a realized tax gain of $14,000 ($21,200 – $7,200). In this case, $12,400 will be allocated to Sally.

	Total	Sally	John
Realized gain	$14,000		
Built-in Gain	$10,800	10,800	
To be split	$ 3,200	1,600	1,600
Gain taxable to each partner		$12,400	$1,600

Reconciliation of Capital Accounts

The partnership may be maintaining two sets of records: one for tax purposes and one for accounting purposes. The tax code requires that Schedule M-1 of Form 1065 reconciles partnership book income or loss to the income or loss reported on the tax return. Schedule M-2 reconciles the partner's balance sheet capital accounts from the beginning of the year to the end of the year.

INCOME AND CREDITS OF PARTNERS (LO 4)

A partner's basis is increased by his or her share of profits. The general rule in determining the partner's share of reported income requires him/her to take into account the distributive share of the partnership's income. The character, such as long-term or short-term capital gain, of any of the items to the partner is the same as it would be to the partnership. The partner then must report the items separately on his/her income tax return, including the impact of the alternative minimum tax. The following is a list of items that are required to be reported separately (IRC 702):

- gains or losses from sales of capital assets,
- gains or losses from sales of IRC 1231 property,
- IRC 179 deductions,
- charitable contributions,
- Dividend and Interest Income (Portfolio Income),
- taxes paid to foreign countries,
- other items provided by regulation.

Partnerships are also required to separately report income from passive activities. The partners must be individually in compliance with the limitations on losses and credits from passive activities. Examples of passive activities include rental activities, limited partnerships, and partnerships or S-corporations where the individual does not materially participate. (Also, see the following discussion concerning passive activities.)

Separately reported items are necessary because certain exclusions and deductions allowed by the tax code can only be taken at the individual-taxpayer level. For instance, an individual and not a partnership can only claim exemptions for dependents. Individuals can offset gross income with losses on long-term capital assets up to $3,000 per year. The unused losses are subject to carry-forward provisions with the $3,000 annual limitations on offsetting ordinary income while awaiting additional long-term gains of the sale of capital assets. Capital gains are subject to tax rates different than those associated with ordinary income.

Another example is that the tax code allows taxpayers to deduct all or part of the cost of certain assets under IRC 179. Each partnership will make its own determination of the amount of property eligible for an IRC 179 deduction. The deduction is allocated to each partner who then determines the amount of deduction, if any, he/she is allowed to deduct on his/her personal return. The partner must reduce his/her basis during the current year for any IRC 179 deduction regardless of whether the full amount was deductible by the individual partner. While the details of IRC 179 and the other examples discussed above are beyond the scope of this text, they do provide examples of the complexities of partnership accounting and reporting for tax purposes.

Partner Net Operating Loss Deduction

As with partnership income, partnership net losses for a given tax year are proportionately reported on the individual partner's tax return. The loss can be used to offset any other income, or a net operating loss may be carried back through the partner's individual tax return to a prior year. There are no tax benefits to the partnership for operating losses.

The ability of an individual partner to deduct a loss is affected by the partner's:

- tax basis,
- amount at risk for the partnership activity giving rise to the loss,
- passive income available to offset passive losses.

Separately stated items, such as charitable deductions, that are not included in the computation of partnership loss are in general not subject to the limitation in tax basis. IRC 704(d) provides that if any amount of a partner's share of a partnership loss for a taxable year is disallowed, then a ratable portion of each item of deduction or loss for that partner is disallowed for that year. Therefore, a partner may deduct a ratable share of charitable contributions, within the regulations established for charitable contributions, which have been paid by the partnership, even if the partnership has a loss. An individual partner may carry forward to future years partnership losses that exceed his/her tax basis. For example, assume a partnership that paid $10,000 in charitable contributions has an ordinary loss of ($20,000). A partner has a tax basis of $6,000. This partner would be able to deduct an ordinary loss of ($4,000) and charitable contributions of ($2,000). The remaining unused ordinary loss and charitable contributions would be subject to carry-forward provisions.

Individual Partner's Income or Loss

The distribution of income to a partner is reported using Schedule K-1 from the partnership's Form 1065. This distributive share is included in the partner's gross income when completing his/her individual Form 1040.

Partners are not considered to be employees of the partnership for purposes of employment taxes. Therefore, each partner who has net income from self-employment, including partnership income, in excess of $400 is responsible for paying the self-employment tax computed based on Schedule SE (Form 1040). The distributive share of income and the impact of the self-employment tax may cause a partner to be required to personally pay quarterly estimated taxes.

Partner's Distributive Share

The partnership agreement governs a partner's distributive share. In situations without an agreement, the distribution will be based upon the partner's interest in the partnership, taking into consideration the facts and circumstances of the situation. In general, allocations that do not conform to the partner's interest must have substantial economic effect (Section 704, 1986 IRS Code).

A partner's distributive share of income can also be modified if the partnership disposes of most types of contributed property within seven years of it having been contributed. An example of precontribution gain on contributed property was discussed earlier.

Limits of Losses

A partner's use of the distributive share of a loss is limited to his/her adjusted basis in the partnership with respect to the year in which the loss is incurred. The adjusted basis is determined without regard to the amount shown in the partnership records in the capital accounts.

A partner with a positive basis in the partnership must have income from sources outside of the partnership to enjoy the benefits of a tax deduction for the losses incurred in the current year. Also, a partner cannot have an adjusted basis less than zero.

Any unused losses are suspended so that the partner can carry forward the loss to a period in which the partner's basis increases. A partner's basis in the partnership may increase through partnership income, by contributing more capital, or by giving a loan to the partnership. These transactions with the partnership should be allowed by the partnership agreement and have a business purpose. For example, contributing capital at the end of year one and having a large withdrawal early in year two might be considered to be a sham transaction by the IRS.

Another method of increasing a partner's adjusted basis is to increase partnership liabilities. This can happen again by having a partner or partners loan funds to the partnership. In addition, the partnership debt may change by increasing year-end current liabilities by either borrowing funds or not making payments to various creditors. The increase in liabilities must be for **amounts-at-risk**. A partner is considered at-risk for (Section 465, 1986 IRS Code):

- amounts contributed,
- borrowed funds for which he/she is personally liable,
- property pledged as security for the amount borrowed.

Passive Activities

Historically, some partnerships were established with the intention of generating losses. These losses were passed through to taxpayers to offset earned income and therefore reduce tax liability. Congress decided these tax shelters were an abuse of the intent of the partnership provisions of the tax code and restricted the recognition of certain losses from certain activities defined as passive activities to eliminate this form of tax avoidance.

A **passive activity** is an activity involving the conduct of a trade or business in which the taxpayer does not materially participate (IRC 469). Passive losses are losses that are generated by passive activities and that can only be offset by passive income. If there is no passive income, then no passive loss can be recognized. Unused passive losses are suspended and carried forward until the taxpayer generates passive income.

By definition, rental activity is considered to be a passive activity. The definition of whether an activity is passive is determined at the partner level; each partner must determine this separately. In addition, each partner must keep track of the amount of passive income and passive loss separately for each activity.

PASSIVE LOSSES

> Understanding whether an activity is passive requires an understanding of the material participation rules. These rules tend to be complex and difficult to understand. An easy-to-understand introduction to this issue can be found by reading "Material Participation and the Effect on Passive Activity Loss Limitations," by Stacy A. Kline, *Strategic Finance*, February 2001, pp. 16 – 17.

PARTNERSHIP DISTRIBUTIONS (LO 5)

In Chapter 1, the accounting for partner withdrawals was discussed. Transferring assets from the partnership to a partner is referred to as a distribution from the partnership. Technically, this distribution, as with withdrawals, is not taken into account when determining a partner's distributive share of partnership income or loss. A partnership distribution can include any of the following:

- a partner withdrawal during the year in anticipation of current-year profits;
- payments to partners during the year, from excess working capital, in anticipation of current-year profits;
- partially or completely liquidating a partner's interest;
- completely liquidating the partnership.

All distributions decrease a partner's basis but not below zero. No gain or loss is recognized by the partnership on the distribution. Consistent with the theory that a partnership is a flow-through entity, the partners do not usually recognize gain or loss on the distribution.

Partnership distributions are classified as either liquidating or non-liquidating. A partner does not recognize a gain unless the distribution is in excess of the partner's basis. Also, a partner does not recognize a loss on a distribution unless it is a **liquidating distribution** (IRC 731). A liquidating distribution is a payment or a series of payments that result in the termination of the partner's interest in the partnership. This can occur when a partnership liquidates by distributing all of its property to the partners or when an individual partner's interest is redeemed by a partnership that then continues to operate.

Non-liquidating distributions, including **partial liquidations** of partnership interest or capital, are considered to be **current distributions**. Any gains or losses recognized are treated as if they were in exchange for an interest in the partnership.

Loss on a Distribution

There are certain exceptions to the rule of partners not recognizing losses on receiving distributions. For instance, during a complete liquidation a loss can be recognized to the extent that the adjusted basis in the partnership exceeds the sum of money and the partner's carryover basis in distributed assets such as unrealized receivables and inventory.

Money as used above includes the fair market value of any marketable securities distributed. Marketable securities are actively traded financial instruments or foreign currencies.

For instance, assume Jane has a 40% profit interest and a $40,000 basis in a partnership. If the partnership has a liquidating distribution to her of $12,000 in cash and inventory with a basis of $20,000, then she can recognize an $8,000 loss.

Generally, if the distributed money represents the partnership's current-year earnings, then there is no gain. The distribution will decrease the basis. However, the current-year share of earnings represent an equivalent offsetting increase in basis. James has a 30% profit interest when the partnership earned $100,000. He received a $30,000 distribution. This results in an increase in his capital account for the earnings $30,000 (30% * 100,000) and a decrease for the distribution $30,000 resulting in a net no change in his capital account.

Distributing Property Other than Money

Distributions may include assets other than money. In this case, if assets such as land, buildings, or automobiles were distributed to a partner, the general rule is that no gain or loss will be immediately recognized. However, if there is any gain or loss inherent in the property when it is distributed, it is deferred until the receiving partner sells the property. For instance, a piece of land with a cost to the partnership (basis) of $10,000 is distributed to a partner, Joan, when the land has a fair market value of $30,000. Neither Joan nor the partnership recognizes a gain on the distribution. Joan has a basis in the land of $10,000, the partnership's basis.

Partnership accounting for the distribution of property must take into account the concept that the entity is not allowed to shift income between partners. Therefore, accounting for the distributions must consider the allocation of precontribution gains and assure that all partners are treated equitably. The regulations provide for methods to properly handle disproportionate distributions of certain assets between partners. These details are beyond the scope of this text.

Impact on Partnership

The partnership distribution of assets, including money, to the partners does not generally result in a taxable event. However, tax consequences can result from transactions that are in fact a sale or exchange with a partner. Partners that engage in transactions with the partnership, other than in their capacity as partners, will be treated as if they are not partners (IRC 707). For example, April and Leo are partners in *A&L* CPAs. In their capacity as partners, they deal with clients. If, however, the partnership had some excess computer equipment and sold it to Leo, this would be treated as a sale to an individual outside of the partnership.

Exceptions to the General Rule of Non-Recognition for Distributions

There are some exceptions to the general rule that a distribution will not result in the recognition of a gain or loss. Some areas where income may be recognized include distributions of:

- property with a precontribution gain,
- unrealized receivables,

- substantially appreciated inventory,
- property subject to a liability.

An example previously discussed was property with a precontribuition gain. Property transferred within seven years of contributing the property, to either the contributing partner or another partner, can result in recognition of gain.

Distributions of unrealized receivables and substantially appreciated non-capital assets such as inventory can result in the recognition of ordinary income (IRC 751). Unrealized receivables can result from a cash basis partnership that has the right to receive payment for goods delivered or services rendered. The partnership has not previously recognized income prior to distribution of the receivable to the partner. Substantially appreciated inventory refers to the inventory where total inventory value has increased in excess of 20% and not just an explicit item valued on its own. For instance, a business has $100,000 of inventory, and one item which has a cost of $100 appreciates to $125. While this item has appreciated more than 20%, the total inventory has not appreciated. If, on the other hand, the total inventory with a cost of $100,000 appreciates to $121,000, then all of the inventory items are treated as appreciated inventory.

Distributions of property subject to a liability are treated as a **deemed distribution of money**. A deemed distribution of money means that the property may be treated for tax purposes as if cash were distributed rather than the property. Therefore, income may be recognized for tax purposes. The partner's share of liabilities is reduced and may trigger a gain if the distribution exceeds the partner's resulting basis. The following is an example of computing the basis of a partner receiving a distribution of property encumbered by a liability.

Pauline and Carol are equal partners with a capital balance of $80,000 each. The partnership owns property valued at $15,000, which also has a basis of $15,000. The property is subject to a $12,000 mortgage. The partnership distributes the property and liability to Pauline. Pauline's new basis is $71,000.

Basis prior to the distribution:	$80,000
Less: Decrease in Partnership Liabilities	
(50% * $12,000)	(6,000)
Plus: Liabilities Assumed	12,000
Less: Property Distribution	(15,000)
Adjusted Partnership Basis	$71,000

Transactions Between Partnership and Partners

There are some limitations on transactions between the partnership and the partner. A transaction that can be characterized as occurring between a partnership and a partner not acting within the capacity of a partner will be treated as occurring with an individual outside of the partnership. These transactions could be treated as sales or exchanges of goods or services, or loans to a partner as mentioned above.

Money loaned to a partner is not considered to be a distribution, but it does decrease the partner's basis. A partner must have an obligation to repay the loan. Interest is either explicitly stated or imputed according to tax rules. A loan is considered to be a **transaction between the partnership and the partner not acting in the capacity of a partner**. Advances or drawings against an individual partner's share of future distributions of income are not loans but are considered distributions made on the last day of the partnership's tax year.

An accrual basis partnership cannot deduct any business expense owed to a cash basis partner until the amount is paid. April loans *A&L* $10,000 with a 10% interest rate. At the end of the year, the partnership accrues interest expense of $1,000, but no payment is made to April. The $1,000 is not a business expense to *A&L* until it is paid.

This rule does not apply to **guaranteed payments**. Guaranteed payments are determined without regard to the income of the partnership (IRC 707). While guaranteed payments are deducted as expenses in determining partnership net income, they are also treated as part of the partner's distributive share of ordinary income.

An example of a guaranteed payment could be a minimum payment required by a partnership agreement. For instance, the *A&L* partnership agreement could require that Sheri should receive 20% of partnership income but not less than $10,000. Remember that the partners' income-sharing ratio is April 40%, Leo 40%, and Sheri 20%. The $10,000 is a minimum payment without regard to partnership income. Assume that partnership income is $40,000. In this situation, Sheri's share without regard to the minimum is $8,000 ($40,000 * 20%). The guaranteed payment is $2,000 ($10,000 – $8,000). Sheri's distribution is $10,000. The remaining $30,000 is reported as distributed income by April and Leo, based upon their proportional shares under the partnership agreement of $15,000 each.

Guaranteed payments are reported by the partnership on line 10 of Form 1065. They are reported to the partners on Schedule K-1. The partners include the information on Schedule E of Form 1040. The partner must include guaranteed payments in income during the partner's tax year in which the partnership tax year ends. For instance, assume the partnership tax year ends on October 31, 20x2. Partner A is a calendar-year taxpayer. The partner will report in 20x2 income guaranteed payments for November and December 20x1 along with guaranteed payments for January 20x2 through October 20x2. The last two months of 2002 will be included in partner A's 2003 return.

Under certain circumstances, a partnership may treat premiums for health insurance paid on behalf of a partner as a guaranteed payment. In this situation, the partnership would deduct the premium paid as an expense. The partners would treat the premium as part of their gross income.

■ CONCEPTUAL QUESTION AND REFLECTION

> *A&L*'s partners are thinking of specifying that the partnership agreement require that the Interest on Capital Balance be paid to the partners regardless of earnings. As their CPA, do you recommend this potential amendment to *A&L*'s partnership agreement?

Termination of a Partnership

Liquidating and non-liquidating distributions were discussed previously. A liquidating distribution results in a partner terminating his interest with the partnership. A partnership itself, however, is assumed to continue unless it is terminated. A partnership is considered to be terminated if (IRC 708):

- no part of any business, financial operation, or venture of the partnership continues to be carried on by any of its partners in a partnership, or
- within a 12-month period there is a sale or exchange of 50% or more of the total interest in partnership capital or profits (**constructive termination** or a **technical termination**).

There are special rules for the merger or consolidation of two or more partnerships or the division of an existing partnership.

Situations exist where a partnership has an interest in another partnership. The partnership with an interest in another partnership is referred to as an upper-tier partner having an interest in a lower-tier partnership. If a sale or exchange in an upper-tier partnership results in termination, then the assumption is that the entire interest in the lower-tier partnership is exchanged.

The "50% or more rule" associated with a constructive termination means 50% or more of total capital interest and 50% or more of total profit interest. Therefore, if there is an exchange of 30% of profit interest and 60% of capital interest, then the partnership is not terminated because there is not a sale or exchange of 50% or more of total interest in partnership profits and capital.

Interests sold on different dates are added together to determine the percentages sold or exchanged. Paul, Peter, and Mary have a partnership. On June 1, 20x1, Paul sells a 40% interest of capital and profits to John, and on April 1, 20x2, Peter sells a 40% interest capital and profits to Sean. Then the partnership is terminated on April 1, 20x2, because more than a 50% interest in total partnership profits and capital was sold. However, if John were to sell his 40% interest to Sean, then the partnership is not terminated because only one 40% interest was sold within a 12-month period.

Liquidation of a partner's interest can cause termination of a partnership. Since a partnership requires two or more people, a two-person partnership will be terminated if only one member is left to carry on the business. However, if the withdrawing partner is still receiving payments under a plan of liquidation from the operating business, then the partnership is not considered liquidated.

A general partnership can be converted into a limited partnership, LLP, or an LLC. Converting to these forms of operation will be treated as a nontaxable event and will allow the partnership to continue.

COMPUTE PARTNERSHIP INCOME OR LOSS (LO 6)

During the year, *A&L* had receipts from services for 20x4 of $250,000 and $1,000 in dividends. The disbursements and expenses included:

Partner Health Insurance ($3,000 each)	9,000
Secretary Salary	25,000
Rent	45,000
Depreciation	3,000
Office Supplies	15,000
Postage	4,000
Phone	8,000
Partners' Salary ($36,000 each)	108,000
April's Bonus (10% for 20x4, paid 12/31/x4)	3,000

Capital Balances at the beginning of the year and Profit Interests were:

April	40%	40,000
Leo	40%	30,000
Sheri	20%	20,000

Form **1065** Department of the Treasury Internal Revenue Service		**U.S. Return of Partnership Income** For calendar year 2000, or tax year beginning ...., 2000, and ending ...., 20..... ▶ **See separate instructions.**		OMB No. 1545-0099 **2000**

A Principal business activity CPA	Use the IRS label. Other- wise, print or type.	Name of partnership A&L CPAs	**D** Employer identification number 14 : 1234567
B Principal product or service Prof. Svcs.		Number, street, and room or suite no. If a P.O. box, see page 13 of the instructions. 123 Main Street	**E** Date business started 1/1/x3
C Business code number		City or town, state, and ZIP code Hometown	**F** Total assets (see page 13 of the instructions) $ 131,000

G Check applicable boxes: **(1)** ☐ Initial return **(2)** ☐ Final return **(3)** ☐ Change in address **(4)** ☐ Amended return

H Check accounting method: **(1)** ☒ Cash **(2)** ☐ Accrual **(3)** ☐ Other (specify) ▶ ....3.........

I Number of Schedules K-1. Attach one for each person who was a partner at any time during the tax year ▶ ...3...

Caution: *Include **only** trade or business income and expenses on lines 1a through 22 below. See the instructions for more information.*

Income

1a Gross receipts or sales		**1a**		
b Less returns and allowances		**1b**	**1c**	250,000
2 Cost of goods sold (Schedule A, line 8)			**2**	
3 Gross profit. Subtract line 2 from line 1c			**3**	
4 Ordinary income (loss) from other partnerships, estates, and trusts *(attach schedule)*			**4**	
5 Net farm profit (loss) *(attach Schedule F (Form 1040))*			**5**	
6 Net gain (loss) from Form 4797, Part II, line 18			**6**	
7 Other income (loss) *(attach schedule)*			**7**	
8 **Total income (loss).** Combine lines 3 through 7			**8**	250,000

Deductions (see page 14 of the instructions for limitations)

9 Salaries and wages (other than to partners) (less employment credits)			**9**	25,000
10 Guaranteed payments to partners			**10**	9,000
11 Repairs and maintenance			**11**	
12 Bad debts			**12**	
13 Rent			**13**	45,000
14 Taxes and licenses			**14**	
15 Interest			**15**	
16a Depreciation (if required, attach Form 4562)		**16a**		
b Less depreciation reported on Schedule A and elsewhere on return		**16b**	**16c**	3,000
17 Depletion **(Do not deduct oil and gas depletion.)**			**17**	
18 Retirement plans, etc.			**18**	
19 Employee benefit programs			**19**	
20 Other deductions *(attach schedule)*			**20**	27,000
21 **Total deductions.** Add the amounts shown in the far right column for lines 9 through 20			**21**	109,000
22 **Ordinary income (loss)** from trade or business activities. Subtract line 21 from line 8			**22**	141,000

Sign Here

Under penalties of perjury, I declare that I have examined this return, including accompanying schedules and statements, and to the best of my knowledge and belief, it is true, correct, and complete. Declaration of preparer (other than general partner or limited liability company member) is based on all information of which preparer has any knowledge.

▶ Signature of general partner or limited liability company member	▶ Date

Paid Preparer's Use Only	Preparer's signature ▶	Date		Check if self-employed ▶ ☐	Preparer's SSN or PTIN
	Firm's name (or yours if self-employed), address, and ZIP code ▶			EIN ▶	
				Phone no. ( )	

For Paperwork Reduction Act Notice, see separate instructions.   Cat. No. 11390Z   Form **1065** (2000)

Form 1065 (2000)   Page **2**

Schedule A   Cost of Goods Sold (see page 17 of the instructions)

1	Inventory at beginning of year	1	
2	Purchases less cost of items withdrawn for personal use	2	
3	Cost of labor	3	
4	Additional section 263A costs (attach schedule)	4	
5	Other costs (attach schedule)	5	
6	**Total.** Add lines 1 through 5	6	
7	Inventory at end of year	7	
8	**Cost of goods sold.** Subtract line 7 from line 6. Enter here and on page 1, line 2	8	

9a Check all methods used for valuing closing inventory:
  (i) ☐ Cost as described in Regulations section 1.471-3
  (ii) ☐ Lower of cost or market as described in Regulations section 1.471-4
  (iii) ☐ Other (specify method used and attach explanation) ▶ ------------------------------
  b Check this box if there was a writedown of "subnormal" goods as described in Regulations section 1.471-2(c). . . . ▶ ☐
  c Check this box if the LIFO inventory method was adopted this tax year for any goods (if checked, attach Form 970) . . ▶ ☐
  d Do the rules of section 263A (for property produced or acquired for resale) apply to the partnership? . . . ☐ **Yes**   ☐ **No**
  e Was there any change in determining quantities, cost, or valuations between opening and closing inventory? ☐ **Yes**   ☐ **No**
     If "Yes," attach explanation.

Schedule B   Other Information

		Yes	No
1	What type of entity is filing this return? Check the applicable box:		

  a ☒ Domestic general partnership   **b** ☐ Domestic limited partnership
  c ☐ Domestic limited liability company   **d** ☐ Domestic limited liability partnership
  e ☐ Foreign partnership   **f** ☐ Other ▶ ------------------

		Yes	No
2	Are any partners in this partnership also partnerships?		X
3	During the partnership's tax year, did the partnership own any interest in another partnership or in any foreign entity that was disregarded as an entity separate from its owner under Regulations sections 301.7701-2 and 301.7701-3? If yes, see instructions for required attachment		X
4	Is this partnership subject to the consolidated audit procedures of sections 6221 through 6233? If "Yes," see **Designation of Tax Matters Partner** below	X	
5	Does this partnership meet **all three** of the following requirements?		
a	The partnership's total receipts for the tax year were less than $250,000;		
b	The partnership's total assets at the end of the tax year were less than $600,000; **and**		
c	Schedules K-1 are filed with the return and furnished to the partners on or before the due date (including extensions) for the partnership return.		
	If "Yes," the partnership is not required to complete Schedules L, M-1, and M-2; Item F on page 1 of Form 1065; or Item J on Schedule K-1		
6	Does this partnership have any foreign partners?		X
7	Is this partnership a publicly traded partnership as defined in section 469(k)(2)?		X
8	Has this partnership filed, or is it required to file, **Form 8264,** Application for Registration of a Tax Shelter?		X
9	At any time during calendar year 2000, did the partnership have an interest in or a signature or other authority over a financial account in a foreign country (such as a bank account, securities account, or other financial account)? See page 19 of the instructions for exceptions and filing requirements for Form TD F 90-22.1. If "Yes," enter the name of the foreign country. ▶ --------------------		X
10	During the tax year, did the partnership receive a distribution from, or was it the grantor of, or transferor to, a foreign trust? If "Yes," the partnership may have to file Form 3520. See page 19 of the instructions		X
11	Was there a distribution of property or a transfer (e.g., by sale or death) of a partnership interest during the tax year? If "Yes," you may elect to adjust the basis of the partnership's assets under section 754 by attaching the statement described under **Elections Made By the Partnership** on page 7 of the instructions		X
12	Enter the number of Forms 8865 attached to this return ▶ 0		

Designation of Tax Matters Partner (see page 19 of the instructions)
Enter below the general partner designated as the tax matters partner (TMP) for the tax year of this return:

Name of designated TMP ▶ April Flowers   Identifying number of TMP ▶ 799-99-9999
Address of designated TMP ▶ 123 Main Street
                             Hometown

Form **1065** (2000)

Schedule K	Partners' Shares of Income, Credits, Deductions, etc.		
	(a) Distributive share items		**(b) Total amount**

Income (Loss)	**1** Ordinary income (loss) from trade or business activities (page 1, line 22)		**1**	141,000
	2 Net income (loss) from rental real estate activities *(attach Form 8825)*		**2**	
	3a Gross income from other rental activities	**3a**		
	b Expenses from other rental activities *(attach schedule)*	**3b**		
	c Net income (loss) from other rental activities. Subtract line 3b from line 3a		**3c**	
	4 Portfolio income (loss): **a** Interest income		**4a**	
	b Ordinary dividends		**4b**	1,000
	c Royalty income		**4c**	
	d Net short-term capital gain (loss) *(attach Schedule D (Form 1065))*		**4d**	
	e Net long-term capital gain (loss) *(attach Schedule D (Form 1065))*:			
	(1) 28% rate gain (loss) ▶ .... **(2)** Total for year . . . . ▶		**4e(2)**	
	f Other portfolio income (loss) *(attach schedule)*		**4f**	
	5 Guaranteed payments to partners		**5**	9,000
	6 Net section 1231 gain (loss) (other than due to casualty or theft) *(attach Form 4797)* . . .		**6**	
	7 Other income (loss) *(attach schedule)*		**7**	
Deductions	**8** Charitable contributions *(attach schedule)*		**8**	
	9 Section 179 expense deduction *(attach Form 4562)*		**9**	
	10 Deductions related to portfolio income (itemize)		**10**	
	11 Other deductions *(attach schedule)*		**11**	
Credits	**12a** Low-income housing credit:			
	(1) From partnerships to which section 42(j)(5) applies for property placed in service before 1990 .		**12a(1)**	
	(2) Other than on line 12a(1) for property placed in service before 1990		**12a(2)**	
	(3) From partnerships to which section 42(j)(5) applies for property placed in service after 1989		**12a(3)**	
	(4) Other than on line 12a(3) for property placed in service after 1989		**12a(4)**	
	b Qualified rehabilitation expenditures related to rental real estate activities *(attach Form 3468)*		**12b**	
	c Credits (other than credits shown on lines 12a and 12b) related to rental real estate activities		**12c**	
	d Credits related to other rental activities		**12d**	
	13 Other credits		**13**	
Investment Interest	**14a** Interest expense on investment debts		**14a**	
	b (1) Investment income included on lines 4a, 4b, 4c, and 4f above		**14b(1)**	1,000
	(2) Investment expenses included on line 10 above		**14b(2)**	
Self-Employment	**15a** Net earnings (loss) from self-employment		**15a**	150,000
	b Gross farming or fishing income		**15b**	
	c Gross nonfarm income		**15c**	
Adjustments and Tax Preference Items	**16a** Depreciation adjustment on property placed in service after 1986		**16a**	
	b Adjusted gain or loss		**16b**	
	c Depletion (other than oil and gas)		**16c**	
	d (1) Gross income from oil, gas, and geothermal properties		**16d(1)**	
	(2) Deductions allocable to oil, gas, and geothermal properties		**16d(2)**	
	e Other adjustments and tax preference items *(attach schedule)*		**16e**	
Foreign Taxes	**17a** Name of foreign country or U.S. possession ▶			
	b Gross income sourced at partner level		**17b**	
	c Foreign gross income sourced at partnership level:			
	(1) Passive ▶ .... **(2)** Listed categories *(attach schedule)* ▶ .... **(3)** General limitation ▶		**17c(3)**	
	d Deductions allocated and apportioned at partner level:			
	(1) Interest expense ▶ .... **(2)** Other . . . . ▶		**17d(2)**	
	e Deductions allocated and apportioned at partnership level to foreign source income:			
	(1) Passive ▶ .... **(2)** Listed categories *(attach schedule)* ▶ .... **(3)** General limitation ▶		**17e(3)**	
	f Total foreign taxes (check one): ▶ Paid ☐ Accrued ☐		**17f**	
	g Reduction in taxes available for credit and gross income from all sources *(attach schedule)* . .		**17g**	
Other	**18** Section 59(e)(2) expenditures: **a** Type ▶ .... **b** Amount ▶		**18b**	
	19 Tax-exempt interest income		**19**	
	20 Other tax-exempt income		**20**	
	21 Nondeductible expenses		**21**	
	22 Distributions of money (cash and marketable securities)		**22**	111,000
	23 Distributions of property other than money		**23**	
	24 Other items and amounts required to be reported separately to partners *(attach schedule)* . . .			

Form 1065 (2000) Page **4**

Analysis of Net Income (Loss)

1 Net income (loss). Combine Schedule K, lines 1 through 7 in column (b). From the result, subtract the sum of Schedule K, lines 8 through 11, 14a, 17f, and 18b . . . . **1** | 151,000

2 Analysis by partner type:	**(i)** Corporate	**(ii)** Individual (active)	**(iii)** Individual (passive)	**(iv)** Partnership	**(v)** Exempt organization	**(vi)** Nominee/Other
a General partners		151,000				
b Limited partners						

Schedule L — Balance Sheets per Books (Not required if Question 5 on Schedule B is answered "Yes.")

Assets	Beginning of tax year (a)	(b)	End of tax year (c)	(d)
1 Cash		40,000		60,000
2a Trade notes and accounts receivable				
b Less allowance for bad debts		30,000		35,000
3 Inventories				
4 U.S. government obligations				
5 Tax-exempt securities				
6 Other current assets (attach schedule)				
7 Mortgage and real estate loans				
8 Other investments (attach schedule)		20,000		24,000
9a Buildings and other depreciable assets	21,000		21,000	
b Less accumulated depreciation	6,000	15,000	9,000	12,000
10a Depletable assets				
b Less accumulated depletion				
11 Land (net of any amortization)				
12a Intangible assets (amortizable only)				
b Less accumulated amortization				
13 Other assets (attach schedule)				
14 Total assets		105,000		131,000
Liabilities and Capital				
15 Accounts payable		15,000		10,000
16 Mortgages, notes, bonds payable in less than 1 year				
17 Other current liabilities (attach schedule)				
18 All nonrecourse loans				
19 Mortgages, notes, bonds payable in 1 year or more				
20 Other liabilities (attach schedule)				
21 Partners' capital accounts		90,000		121,000
22 Total liabilities and capital		105,000		131,000

Schedule M-1 — Reconciliation of Income (Loss) per Books With Income (Loss) per Return
(Not required if Question 5 on Schedule B is answered "Yes." See page 30 of the instructions.)

1 Net income (loss) per books	142,000	**6** Income recorded on books this year not included on Schedule K, lines 1 through 7 (itemize):
2 Income included on Schedule K, lines 1 through 4, 6, and 7, not recorded on books this year (itemize):		**a** Tax-exempt interest $
3 Guaranteed payments (other than health insurance)		**7** Deductions included on Schedule K, lines 1 through 11, 14a, 17f, and 18b, not charged against book income this year (itemize):
4 Expenses recorded on books this year not included on Schedule K, lines 1 through 11, 14a, 17f, and 18b (itemize):		**a** Depreciation $
a Depreciation $		
b Travel and entertainment $		**8** Add lines 6 and 7
5 Add lines 1 through 4	142,000	**9** Income (loss) (Analysis of Net Income (Loss), line 1). Subtract line 8 from line 5	142,000

Schedule M-2 — Analysis of Partners' Capital Accounts (Not required if Question 5 on Schedule B is answered "Yes.")

1 Balance at beginning of year	90,000	**6** Distributions: **a** Cash	111,000
2 Capital contributed during year		**b** Property
3 Net income (loss) per books	142,000	**7** Other decreases (itemize):
4 Other increases (itemize):		**8** Add lines 6 and 7
5 Add lines 1 through 4	232,000	**9** Balance at end of year. Subtract line 8 from line 5	121,000

Form **1065** (2000)

SCHEDULE K-1 (Form 1065) Department of the Treasury Internal Revenue Service	**Partner's Share of Income, Credits, Deductions, etc.** ▶ See separate instructions. For calendar year 2000 or tax year beginning , 2000, and ending , 20	OMB No. 1545-0099 **2000**

Partner's identifying number ▶ | **Partnership's identifying number** ▶

Partner's name, address, and ZIP code	Partnership's name, address, and ZIP code
April Flowers 1 Garden Blvd. Hometown, USA 11111	A&L CPAs 123 Main St. Hometown, USA 11111

A This partner is a ☒ general partner ☐ limited partner
☐ limited liability company member
B What type of entity is this partner? ▶ _Individual_
C Is this partner a ☐ domestic or a ☐ foreign partner?
D Enter partner's percentage of:

	(i) Before change or termination	**(ii)** End of year
Profit sharing	%	_40_ %
Loss sharing	%	_40_ %
Ownership of capital	%	_40_ %

E IRS Center where partnership filed return:

F Partner's share of liabilities (see instructions):
Nonrecourse . . . . $ _____
Qualified nonrecourse financing . . $ _____
Other . . . . $ _4,000_
G Tax shelter registration number . ▶ _____
H Check here if this partnership is a publicly traded partnership as defined in section 469(k)(2) . . . . . ☐
I Check applicable boxes: **(1)** ☐ Final K-1 **(2)** ☐ Amended K-1

J Analysis of partner's capital account:

(a) Capital account at beginning of year	**(b)** Capital contributed during year	**(c)** Partner's share of lines 3, 4, and 7, Form 1065, Schedule M-2	**(d)** Withdrawals and distributions	**(e)** Capital account at end of year (combine columns (a) through (d))
40,000		56,800	(39,000)	

(a) Distributive share item		**(b)** Amount	**(c)** 1040 filers enter the amount in column (b) on:
1 Ordinary income (loss) from trade or business activities . . .	**1**	56,400	See page 6 of Partner's Instructions for Schedule K-1 (Form 1065).
2 Net income (loss) from rental real estate activities	**2**		
3 Net income (loss) from other rental activities	**3**		
4 Portfolio income (loss):			
a Interest	**4a**		Sch. B, Part I, line 1
b Ordinary dividends	**4b**	400	Sch. B, Part II, line 5
c Royalties	**4c**		Sch. E, Part I, line 4
d Net short-term capital gain (loss)	**4d**		Sch. D, line 5, col. (f)
e Net long-term capital gain (loss):			
(1) 28% rate gain (loss)	**4e(1)**		Sch. D, line 12, col. (g)
(2) Total for year.	**4e(2)**		Sch. D, line 12, col. (f)
f Other portfolio income (loss) *(attach schedule)*	**4f**		Enter on applicable line of your return.
5 Guaranteed payments to partner	**5**	3,000	See page 6 of Partner's Instructions for Schedule K-1 (Form 1065).
6 Net section 1231 gain (loss) (other than due to casualty or theft) .	**6**		
7 Other income (loss) *(attach schedule)*	**7**		Enter on applicable line of your return.
8 Charitable contributions (see instructions) *(attach schedule)* . .	**8**		Sch. A, line 15 or 16
9 Section 179 expense deduction.	**9**		See pages 7 and 8 of Partner's Instructions for Schedule K-1 (Form 1065).
10 Deductions related to portfolio income *(attach schedule)* . . .	**10**		
11 Other deductions *(attach schedule)*.	**11**		
12a Low-income housing credit:			
(1) From section 42(j)(5) partnerships for property placed in service before 1990	**12a(1)**		
(2) Other than on line 12a(1) for property placed in service before 1990	**12a(2)**		
(3) From section 42(j)(5) partnerships for property placed in service after 1989	**12a(3)**		Form 8586, line 5
(4) Other than on line 12a(3) for property placed in service after 1989	**12a(4)**		
b Qualified rehabilitation expenditures related to rental real estate activities	**12b**		
c Credits (other than credits shown on lines 12a and 12b) related to rental real estate activities.	**12c**		See page 8 of Partner's Instructions for Schedule K-1 (Form 1065).
d Credits related to other rental activities	**12d**		
13 Other credits	**13**		

Income (Loss) — lines 1–7
Deductions — lines 8–11
Credits — lines 12a–13

For Paperwork Reduction Act Notice, see Instructions for Form 1065.   Cat. No. 11394R   **Schedule K-1 (Form 1065) 2000**

(a) Distributive share item		(b) Amount	(c) 1040 filers enter the amount in column (b) on:
Investment Interest	**14a** Interest expense on investment debts	**14a**	Form 4952, line 1
	b **(1)** Investment income included on lines 4a, 4b, 4c, and 4f . .	**14b(1)** 400	See page 9 of Partner's Instructions for Schedule K-1 (Form 1065).
	(2) Investment expenses included on line 10	**14b(2)**	
Self-employment	**15a** Net earnings (loss) from self-employment	**15a** 59,400	Sch. SE, Section A or B
	b Gross farming or fishing income.	**15b**	See page 9 of Partner's Instructions for Schedule K-1 (Form 1065).
	c Gross nonfarm income.	**15c**	
Adjustments and Tax Preference Items	**16a** Depreciation adjustment on property placed in service after 1986	**16a**	See page 9 of Partner's Instructions for Schedule K-1 (Form 1065) and Instructions for Form 6251.
	b Adjusted gain or loss	**16b**	
	c Depletion (other than oil and gas)	**16c**	
	d **(1)** Gross income from oil, gas, and geothermal properties . .	**16d(1)**	
	(2) Deductions allocable to oil, gas, and geothermal properties	**16d(2)**	
	e Other adjustments and tax preference items *(attach schedule)*	**16e**	
Foreign Taxes	**17a** Name of foreign country or U.S. possession ▶ -----------------		
	b Gross income sourced at partner level	**17b**	
	c Foreign gross income sourced at partnership level:		
	(1) Passive	**17c(1)**	
	(2) Listed categories *(attach schedule)*	**17c(2)**	
	(3) General limitation	**17c(3)**	
	d Deductions allocated and apportioned at partner level:		Form 1116, Part I
	(1) Interest expense	**17d(1)**	
	(2) Other	**17d(2)**	
	e Deductions allocated and apportioned at partnership level to foreign source income:		
	(1) Passive	**17e(1)**	
	(2) Listed categories *(attach schedule)*	**17e(2)**	
	(3) General limitation	**17e(3)**	
	f Total foreign taxes (check one): ▶ ☐ Paid ☐ Accrued . . .	**17f**	Form 1116, Part II
	g Reduction in taxes available for credit and gross income from all sources *(attach schedule)*	**17g**	See Instructions for Form 1116.
Other	**18** Section 59(e)(2) expenditures: **a** Type ▶ -----------------		See page 9 of Partner's Instructions for Schedule K-1 (Form 1065).
	b Amount	**18b**	
	19 Tax-exempt interest income	**19**	Form 1040, line 8b
	20 Other tax-exempt income	**20**	See pages 9 and 10 of Partner's Instructions for Schedule K-1 (Form 1065).
	21 Nondeductible expenses	**21**	
	22 Distributions of money (cash and marketable securities) . . .	**22** 39,000	
	23 Distributions of property other than money	**23**	
	24 Recapture of low-income housing credit:		
	a From section 42(j)(5) partnerships	**24a**	Form 8611, line 8
	b Other than on line 24a	**24b**	
Supplemental Information	**25** Supplemental information required to be reported separately to each partner *(attach additional schedules if more space is needed):*		

SUMMARY

The **Learning Objectives** for this chapter were:

- Explain how tax laws define partners and partnerships.
- Discuss tax consequences of the formation of a partnership.
- Compute a partner's tax basis.
- Compute a partner's share of income or loss items.
- Explain the tax impact of a partnership distribution.
- Compute partnership income or loss.

Explain how tax laws define partners and partnerships.

The tax code defines a partnership as an unincorporated organization that includes more than one individual. A partnership provides taxpayers with the ability to transact business in a flexible manner without being taxed at the entity level. Alternative pass-through entities recognized under tax law include LLCs, LLPs, and S-corporations.

Discuss tax consequences of the formation of a partnership.

The partnership is not a taxable entity. Elections made at the partnership level include:

- depreciation methods,
- capitalizing or expensing qualified business expenses,
- basis adjustment of certain partnership property, and
- tax audits.

Compute a partner's tax basis.

A partner's tax basis is based upon the cost of the asset contributed. This does not have to equal the fair market value of the asset that is used to determine the partner's capital contribution. Records must be kept related to both the partner's capital interest and tax basis. Liabilities contributed with assets that are assumed by the partnership are treated the same as if there had been a distribution to the contributing partner.

Precontribution gains or losses on contributed property can result in taxable gains to the contributing partner upon sale or distribution of the property by the partnership. John and Sally were used as an example where Sally was not able to shift income associated with the contribution of an overvalued asset to the J&S partnership.

Compute a partner's share of income or loss items.

For income tax purposes, a partner must take into account separately the distributive share of the partnership's income. The character of any item to the partner is the same as how it was realized or incurred by the partnership. The partner, then, must report separately on his/her income tax return, including the impact of the alternative minimum tax, items such as:

- gains or losses from sales of capital assets,
- gains or losses from sales of IRC 1231 property,
- charitable contributions,
- dividends,
- taxes paid to foreign countries,
- other items provided by regulation,
- passive activities.

Explain the tax impact of a partnership distribution.

A distribution is a transfer of assets from the partnership to a partner. This distribution is not taken into account when determining a partner's distributive share of partnership income or loss. The partner's basis is decreased, but not below zero, by all distributions. The partnership does not recognize gain or loss on the distribution. A partnership distribution can include any of the following:

- a partner withdrawal during the year in anticipation of current-year profits;
- payments to partners during the year, from excess working capital, in anticipation of current-year profits;
- partially or completely liquidating a partner's interest;
- completely liquidating the partnership.

Distributions of property subject to a liability are treated as a distribution of money. Pauline and Carol were used as an example to compute a partner's new basis when property with a liability is distributed to a partner.

Transactions can occur between a partnership and an individual partner not acting with the capacity of a partner. These transactions can create a loan to or from the partner. Guaranteed payments are determined without regard to partnership income and are treated as part of the partner's distributive share of ordinary income.

A partnership is assumed to continue unless it is terminated. A partnership is terminated if no part of the business continues to be carried on or a constructive termination occurs when a 50% exchange of interest takes place within a 12-month period.

Compute partnership income or loss.

A partial Form 1065 partnership tax return was completed for *A&L*.

QUESTIONS

1. How is partnership income taxed?
2. Why might a family partnership be formed?
3. Why would the IRS audit the partnership information at the entity level?
4. A partnership year ends on 11/30/x1. In what tax year would individual partners report their share of this income?
5. The formation of a partnership might include the contribution of appreciated property by a partner. Explain why and how the tax code allows this contribution to be a tax-deferred event.
6. Explain how, upon formation of a partnership, a partner can have a capital account balance of $10,000 and a tax basis in the partnership interest of $5,000.
7. Explain the impact on the basis of each partner's interest if a partnership assumes a mortgage on a building contributed by a new partner.
8. What items can increase a partner's basis?
9. What items can decrease a partner's basis?
10. Why are many partnership income or expense items reported separately to each partner?
11. Briefly discuss the limitations on the deductibility of losses by individual partners due to basis, at-risk, and passive loss provisions.
12. When can a partner recognize a loss on a distribution?
13. What is a guaranteed payment? How does a guaranteed payment affect the calculation of the partnership's ordinary income or loss?

EXERCISES

Exercise 3-1

Multiple Choice—Select the best answer for each of the following.

1. Partnership income to be reported as taxable income by a partner includes:
   a. the partner's share of distributive income only if it is actually distributed to the partner during the year;
   b. the partner's salary and interest payments received by the partner during the year;
   c. the partner's share of distributive income, whether or not it is distributed during the year;
   d. none, because the partnership will report and pay tax on the income.

2. Bart contributes land with a cost to him of $12,000 and a fair market value of $20,000 to the B&B partnership. What will be his basis in the partnership interest and the balance in his capital account at the date of contribution?

	Basis	Capital Account
a.	$20,000	$20,000
b.	$12,000	$12,000
c.	$20,000	$12,000
d.	$12,000	$20,000

3. Bart contributed land two years ago with a basis of $12,000 and a fair market value at that date of $20,000 to the B&B partnership in exchange for a 50% interest in capital and profits and losses. If the asset is sold this year for $24,000, what is the total amount of taxable gain and how much of it will be reportable by Bart?

	Total gain	Bart's share
a.	$12,000	$10,000
b.	$12,000	$6,000
c.	$4,000	$4,000
d.	$4,000	$2,000

4. George could establish a family partnership to share income with his three minor children:
   a. in all circumstances, as long as the partnership was valid under state law.
   b. if the partnership income consisted of George's fees from his medical practice.
   c. if capital was a material income producing factor and the partnership operates for a bona fide business purpose.
   d. never, because minor children cannot be partners.

5. A three-person LLC will be treated for tax purposes:
   a. always as a corporation because the entity affords limited liability to the members.
   b. always as a partnership because the members benefit by flow through taxation.
   c. normally as a partnership; however, the LLC may elect to be classified as a corporation.
   d. as none of the above.

6. Which of the following items can be included as part of the ordinary income that flows through to the partners rather than being reported as a separately stated item?
   a. Charitable contributions.
   b. Long-term capital gains.
   c. Rental property income.
   d. Advertising expense.

7. Rosie's basis in her 40% partnership interest is $18,000 before considering this year's operations. If the partnership incurs a loss for the year of $50,000, what is the proper tax treatment of her share of the loss assuming she is a material participant in the operation of the business and is personally at risk for her entire investment?
   a. $20,000 deductible loss is reported by Rosie.
   b. $18,000 deductible loss is reported by Rosie; the remaining $2,000 loss is never deductible.
   c. $0; losses are not deductible by individual partners.
   d. $18,000 deductible loss is reported by Rosie; the remaining $2,000 loss is suspended and carried forward to future periods.

8. When a partnership increases its debt by borrowing from the bank:
   a. There is no impact on each partner's basis because the transaction is between the bank and the partnership directly.
   b. Each partner's basis will normally increase by his/her share of the debt taken on by the partnership.
   c. Each partner's basis will normally decrease by his/her share of the debt taken on by the partnership.
   d. None of the above.

9. A partnership is considered terminated for tax purposes when:
   a. a 20% partner sells his interest to an unrelated party in the first month of the new tax year.
   b. within a 12-month period, there is a sale or exchange of 50% or more of the total interest in partnership capital or profits.
   c. the cumulative total of interests sold or exchanged exceeds 50%.
   d. the partnership discontinues one of its major lines of business.

10. A partner has a $25,000 basis in his partnership interest immediately before a distribution in complete liquidation of his interest. If he receives cash of $20,000 and inventory with a basis to the partnership of $4,000 and a fair market value of $7,000, what is the tax consequence?
   a. $2,000 taxable gain on the liquidation and a $7,000 basis in the inventory.
   b. No taxable gain or loss and a carryover $4,000 basis in the inventory.
   c. $1,000 taxable loss on the liquidation and a $4,000 basis in the inventory.
   d. $2,000 taxable gain and a $4,000 basis in the inventory.

Exercise 3-2

Formation of Partnership and Basis (LO 2 & 3)

Alexander, Brian and Christopher form a partnership with the following contributions:

	Contribution	Basis	Fair Market Value	Capital & Profits Interest %
Alexander	Cash	$10,000	$10,000	1/3
Brian	Equipment	6,000	10,000	1/3
Christopher	Legal Services	0	10,000	1/3

The legal services were performed by Christopher in drafting the original partnership agreement and other organizational matters.

   a. How much gain (loss) does each of the partners recognize upon formation of the partnership?
   b. What basis does each partner have in his partnership interest?
   c. What basis does the partnership have in each asset?

Exercise 3-3

Formation of Partnership: Explain Difference in Entities (LO 1)

As Christopher, should you discuss with Alexander and Brian the different choices of entities available to them in forming a business?

Exercise 3-4

Formation of Partnership and Basis (LO 1, 2, & 3)

Mia and Brandi form the M&K partnership with the following contributions:

	Contribution	Basis	Fair Market Value	Capital & Profits Interest %
Mia	Cash	$75,000	$ 75,000	75%
Brandi	Building	70,000	115,000	25%

The building has a $90,000 mortgage that is assumed by the partnership. (Assume that the partners will share profits and losses and bear the risk of debt in the ratio of their initial capital contributions.)
  a. What gain or loss is recognized by each partner upon formation of the partnership?
  b. What basis does each partner have in her partnership interest?
  c. What basis does the partnership have in each asset?

Exercise 3-5

Formation of Partnership and Basis (LO 1, 2, & 3)

Respond to Questions a – c from Exercise 4 above under the assumption that the basis of the building that Brandi contributed was only $50,000.

Exercise 3-6

Reportable Share of Income (LO 4)

During the second year of operations, the M&K partnership from Exercise 4 reports ordinary income of $60,000, dividend income of $2,000, and charitable contributions of $4,000. The partnership also repays $5,000 of the mortgage on the building. Assume that Mia and Brandi began year two with partnership basis of $120,000 and $4,000, respectively.
  a. Determine the tax treatment of each partner's share of the reportable income (expense) items.
  b. Calculate the basis each partner will have in the partnership interest at year-end.

Exercise 3-7

Reportable Share of Income (LO 4)

Assume instead that the M&K partnership from Exercises 4–6 reported an ordinary loss from operations of $40,000 for year two dividend income of $2,000. Also, assume again that Mia & Brandi began the year with basis of $120,000 and $4,000, respectively.
  a. Determine the tax treatment of each partner's share of the reportable items.
  b. Calculate the basis each partner will have in her partnership interest at year-end.
  c. What happens to any losses in excess of the basis?
  d. Would there be any tax planning suggestions that you could make in order to allow Brandi to deduct the full amount of her loss for the year?

Exercise 3-8	**Reportable Share of Income (LO 4)**

Certain income or expense items are reported separately to each partner rather than being included in the computation of the partnership ordinary income. In the list below, identify each item that would be separately reported to the partners and briefly explain why separate reporting of that item is necessary:

> Salary expense—office employees
> Charitable contributions
> Depreciation expense
> Cost of goods sold
> IRC 179 deduction
> Interest income (taxable)
> Short-term capital gain
> Rental property loss
> Advertising expense

Exercise 3-9	**Reportable Share of Income (LO 4 & 6)**

The PM partnership is owned 60% by Peter and 40% by Mary. They also share profits and losses in this relationship. The partnership had the following results of operations for the partnership year ended 12/31/x2:

Sales	$250,000
Cost of goods sold	160,000
Office salary expense	50,000
Advertising expense	10,000
Dividend income	1,200
Charitable contributions	1,500
Other operating expenses	18,000

a. What is the ordinary income or (loss) of the partnership for the year?
b. What items would be passed through to Peter and Mary on the Schedule K-1s prepared for the year?

Exercise 3-10	**Reportable Share of Income (LO 4 & 6)**

If in Exercise 9 above the other operating expenses had been $52,000 rather than $18,000 what items and amounts would be reported to each of the partners?

Exercise 3-11	**Reportable Share of Income (LO 4 & 6)**

Refer again to the original information in Exercise 9. In addition to the revenues and expenses listed, Mary was given a guaranteed payment of $34,000 for her services for the year.
a. Under these circumstances what would be the ordinary income or loss of the partnership?
b. What amounts would now be reported by both Peter and Mary?

Exercise 3-12

Distribution of Assets Other than Cash (LO 5)

In the following two independent situations, calculate the partner's: 1. recognized gain or loss, 2. basis in the partnership interest after the distribution, and 3. basis of any non-cash property received by the partner. Assume that there are no precontribution gains or losses to be recognized and that all distributions are pro rata in regard to the IRC 751 assets.

    a. Tony had a $15,000 basis in his partnership interest before receiving a current distribution consisting of cash of $3,000 and land with a basis to the partnership of $10,000 and a fair market value of $16,000.

    b. Ken received a liquidating partnership distribution consisting solely of inventory with a fair market value of $12,000 and a basis to the partnership of $8,000, receivables with a fair market value of $3,000 and a basis of $0, and cash of $2,500. His basis in the partnership interest immediately before the distribution was $20,000.

Exercise 3-13

Distribution of Assets Other than Cash (LO 5)

Alex, Brian, and Christopher own 38%, 10%, and 52% of the ABC partnership, respectively. For each of the following independent scenarios, determine whether the ABC partnership terminates and, if so, on what date does the termination occur?

    a. Alex sells his entire interest to Jeff on April 1, and Jeff resells ½ of this interest to Ken on November 1.

    b. Alex & Brian each receive a liquidating distribution on July 1.

    c. Christopher sells his interest to David on June 15 for a cash down payment and a note with a series of monthly installment payments to be made over the next three years.

    d. Christopher gives his entire interest to his daughter, Diane, on November 1.

PROBLEMS

Problem 3-1

Formation of a Partnership and Basis (LO 1, 2, & 3)

Five individuals decide to form the HiFive partnership. The contributions of each partner and the partnership interest received are listed below. The partners will share the economic risk of loss from any liabilities according to their partnership interests.

Individual	Asset	Basis to Partner	Fair Market Value	Partnership Interest
Jill	Cash	$10,000	$10,000	10%
Jerri	Accounts Receivable	-0-	15,000	15%
Jessica	Office Equipment	17,000	15,000	15%
Joanne	Building	15,000	100,000	50%
Jim	Services	?	10,000	10%

Additional information relative to the contributions:

■ The accounts receivable contributed by Jerri are from a cash basis sole-proprietorship.

■ The office equipment contributed by Jessica had been used by her in her small business and had been depreciated from its original cost of $20,000.

■ The partnership assumes the $50,000 balance remaining on the mortgage on the building contributed by Joanne.

■ Jim provided services in connection with drafting the partnership agreement and filing any paperwork.

a. How much gain, loss, or income must each partner report upon the formation of the partnership?
b. What gain or loss does the partnership recognize?
c. What basis does each partner take in his/her partnership interest?
d. What basis does the partnership have in each asset?
e. If the partnership sells the equipment to a third party for $15,000 shortly after formation, what amount of gain or loss must be recognized and how is it allocated to each partner?

Problem 3-2

Partner's Basis when Acquiring a Share of a Continuing Partnership (LO 3)

Peter purchases a 30% interest in the Falcon partnership on January 1 for $10,000. At that time, he assumes his share of the $10,000 of partnership debt. The partnership incurs a loss of $15,000 for the year ended December 31, and partnership liabilities have increased to $16,000 by year-end.

a. What is Peter's basis in his partnership interest on January 1, the date of purchase?
b. What is his basis December 31, assuming he made no additional contributions or withdrawals during the year?
c. c. If the partnership loss for the year were $60,000 instead of $15,000, what would be Peter's year-end basis?

Problem 3-3

Determining a Partner's Reportable Share of Income (LO 4)

The Racer partnership had the following items of income/(loss) for the current year:

Ordinary income	$40,000
Long-term capital gain	12,000
Short-term capital loss	(8,000)
Charitable contributions	(4,000)
Dividend income	3,000

Assume that each of the items is earned or incurred ratably throughout the year. Ken owned his 40% interest from January 1 through June 30 when he sold the entire interest to Lester for $75,000 (including Lester's assumption of 40% of the partnership debt).

a. What income or loss items will Ken report for the current year?
b. What income or loss items will Lester report?
c. If Ken's basis in the interest was $50,000 on January 1 (including his share of debt) and there were no IRC 751 assets held by the partnership at the date of sale, what amount and what nature of gain would Ken report when he sold the interest to Lester?

Problem 3-4

Distribution to Partners (LO 4)

Mia is a 1/4 partner in the MLS partnership when she receives a liquidating distribution consisting of $15,000 cash and land with a fair market value of $65,000 and a basis of $35,000. There is no precontribution gain associated with the land. Immediately before the distribution, the partnership has only two assets and no liabilities outstanding:

	Basis	Fair Market Value
Cash	$ 80,000	$80,000
Land	130,000	260,000

Mia's basis in her interest was $60,000 immediately before the distribution.

a. What gain or loss does the partnership recognize on the distribution of the land?
b. What gain/(loss) is realized by Mia upon receipt of the distribution? How much must be recognized? What is the nature of the income/(loss)?
c. What basis does Mia take in the land?

Problem 3-5

Distribution to Partners (LO 4)

Assume the same facts from Problem 4, above, except that the second asset is inventory rather than land and the distribution to Mia consists of $15,000 cash and inventory with a Fair Market Value of $65,000 and a basis of $35,000.

    a. What gain or loss must the partnership now recognize?
    b. What gain (loss) does Mia recognize, and what is the nature of the income?
    c. What basis does Mia take in the inventory?

Problem 3-6

Sale of Partnership Property (LO 3 & 4)

Mary had contributed land with a basis of $15,000 and a fair market value of $25,000 for her 20% partnership interest. The PPM partnership held the land for three years and then sold it to an outsider for $32,000. Assume that Mary had held the land as an investment asset prior to contributing it to the partnership.

    a. What amount and type of income will the partnership report upon the sale of this land?
    b. What amount of income and type of income will Mary report concerning this transaction?

Problem 3-7

Guaranteed Payments (LO 3, 4 & 5)

P&P partnership has $20,000 of ordinary partnership income and a $15,000 long-term capital gain before consideration of any guaranteed payments to partners.

    a. If Peter is entitled to a guaranteed payment of $12,000 and the partners share profits and losses equally, what amount of income would be reported for the year by each of the partners, Peter and Paul?
    b. How would your answer to Part a change if the guaranteed payment to Peter was $28,000 rather than $12,000?
    c. If Peter's basis in his partnership interest was $14,000 prior to this year's activity, what is his year-end basis in each of the above scenarios?

Problem 3-8

Distribution of Partnership Property (LO 3, 4, & 5)

Four years ago, Able contributed land with a basis of $9,000 and a fair market value of $15,000 to the AB partnership. In the current year, the partnership distributed the land to Baker. At the date of the distribution, Baker's partnership basis was $40,000 and the fair market value of the land was $18,000. Assume the distribution has no IRC 751 implications.

    a. How much gain does Baker record upon receipt of the land?
    b. Does Able recognize any gain when the land is distributed? If so, how much?
    c. What basis will Baker have in the land?
    d. If instead of distributing the land to Baker it was sold to an outside party for $18,000, how will the gain, if any, be passed through to Able and Baker? Assume they are equal partners.

Problem 3-9

Explain the Advantages of Partnership (LO 1)

From a tax perspective, what are the relative advantages and disadvantages of forming a partnership versus a closely held C-corporation when the owners anticipate losses in the early years of the entity? What if, instead, moderate profits are anticipated and the owners are personally already in the highest individual income tax brackets?

Problem 3-10

Internet Assignment

In Chapter 1, April and Leo formed a partnership. Many CPA firms have structured the organization using legal forms of operation other than a partnership. Examine the website of an international CPA firm and of a local firm to determine how the firms are structured. Based upon your current understanding of the different legal structures available for CPA firms, write a memo to April and Leo recommending a legal form of operation for *A&L*. In responding to April and Leo, you should access and review the Fleischmann and Bryant article as well as the Karl Article referred to in Chapter 1 of the partnership module.

Problem 3-11

Return Preparation Problem (LO 6)

Brad and Chris Culpepper established a landscaping and snowplowing partnership, Flowers & Flakes, several years ago (EI #14-0562500). Each contributed capital equal to their profit and loss percentage and both participate in the ongoing activities of the business. During the busy summer season, they hire seasonal contract help and they have one office person who works year round. The company's office is located at 5 Azure Lane, Saratoga Springs, New York 12235. Brad (Social Security number 122-34-3221) lives at 15 Oakhill Road, Saratoga Springs, New York and is the managing partner with a 60% capital and profits interest. His younger brother Chris (Social Security number 065-33-4543) lives at 807 Main Street, Round Lake, New York and has a 40% capital and profits interest. In addition to Brad's guaranteed payment of $14,000, the brothers took withdrawals during the year of $34,200 and $22,800 for Brad and Chris, respectively.

The partnership performs services for customers and does not maintain any substantial inventories of plants or snowplowing supplies. Customers are usually invoiced immediately after the work is performed. Some of the snowplowing customers with annual contracts pay for the entire season in early January. Flowers & Flakes uses the cash method of accounting for its receipts and disbursements and reports on a calendar-year basis. The partnership has no foreign activities or connections, is not a tax shelter, and has had no changes in ownership during the year. The following table provides the Income Statement for Flowers & Flakes for the current year ended 12/31.

Required:

Prepare the current-year partnership return for Flowers & Flakes partnership. You can omit the preparation of Form 4562 for depreciation and only complete the Schedule K-1 for Brad rather than completing both K-1s. You can download the most recent year's forms and instructions from the IRS website.

Flowers & Flakes Partnership Income Statement
for the Year Ended December 31 of the Current Year:

Landscaping fee receipts		$165,000
Snowplowing fee receipts		60,000
		$225,000
Cost of goods sold:		
Landscaping Plants & Materials	$65,000	
Contract Labor	20,000	(85,000)
Gross Profit		140,000
Expenses:		
Salary to office employee	18,000	
Guaranteed payment to Brad as Managing Partner	14,000	
Truck operating expenses	12,000	
Accounting & legal fees	1,600	

Rent expense	10,250	
Interest expense (plow truck loan)	3,600	
Meals (only 50% deductible)	800	
Depreciation expense—equipment and plow truck on a MACRS basis	8,350	
Charitable contributions—United Way	2,000	
Payroll taxes	1,500	
Health Insurance premiums—($4,000 each for office employee, Brad, and Chris)	12,000	
Total expenses		84,100
Operating Income		55,900
Other Income & Expense:		
Interest Income	1,150	
Short-term capital gain—sale of 100 shares of XY stock	550	1,700
Net Income		$ 57,600

INDEX